I0116786

# IN SEARCH OF THE UNKNOWN

Other books by D. Scott Rogo

*A Casebook of Otherworldly Music*
*A Psychic Study of the Music of the Spheres*
*Methods and Models for Education in Parapsychology*
*The Welcoming Silence*
*An Experience of Phantoms*
*Parapsychology: A Century of Inquiry*
*Exploring Psychic Phenomena*
*The Haunted Universe*
*Mind Beyond the Body*
*Minds and Motion*
*The Haunted House Handbook*
*The Poltergeist Experience*
*Phone Calls from the Dead* (with Raymond Bayless)
*Earth's Secret Inhabitants* (with Jerome Clark)
*The Tujunga Canyon Contacts* (with Ann Druffel)
*UFO Abductions*
*Miracles*
*ESP and Your Pet*
*Leaving the Body*
*Our Psychic Potentials*
*The Search for Yesterday*
*Life after Death*
*Mind over Matter*

# In Search of the Unknown

## The Odyssey of a Psychical Investigator

By D. Scott Rogo

Anomalist Books
*San Antonio • New York*

**In Search of the Unknown**
Copyright © 1976 by D. Scott Rogo

Anomalist Books edition: 2005
ISBN: 1933665068

Originally published by Taplinger Publishing Company.
Reprinted with permission of the Rogo Family Trust.

Back cover author biography based on George P. Hansen's
"D. Scott Rogo and His Contributions to Parapsychology"
at tricksterbook.com.

Cover image: Alexander Briel Perez

Cover design by Ansen Seale

All rights reserved, including the right to reproduce
this book or portions thereof in any form whatsoever.
For information, go to anomalistbooks.com or write to:

Anomalist Books
5150 Broadway #108
San Antonio, TX 78209

Anomalist Books
PO Box 577
Jefferson Valley, NY 10535

To my Mother

## Author's Note

Occasionally in this book I have changed the names of some of the people, and very occasionally the name of the town where they lived, to insure their privacy.

# Acknowledgments

During the course of a career, one becomes indebted to several people without whose help success would never have been achieved. It is fitting that in this chronicle of my own psychic odyssey I should acknowledge individually those who aided my various endeavors. First, to Mr. Raymond Bayless without whose encouragement I might never have devoted myself full-time to parapsychology. In this respect, I would like to acknowledge the support of Mrs. Barbara Smith and Mrs. Clarissa Plantamura (now Mulders) who also helped me so much in my first explorations. To Mary and Curtis Fuller of *Fate* magazine who published my first articles and reports and Mr. James Bolen of *Psychic*, all of whom encouraged me not only as an investigator but as a writer as well. To the Parapsychology Foundation, especially Mr. and Mrs. Robert Coly and Mr. Allan Angoff, who have supported my work, both morally and financially, heartfelt thanks are due. To Dr. Robert Morris who has counseled me so expertly on various problems arising from psychical research. Special thanks are offered to the many psychics who have donated their time for this work and some of whom have become personal friends, especially Mr. Stuart Blue Harary and Mr. Attila von Szalay. Finally, credit is due to the wise counseling of my editor, Miss Bobs Pinkerton, whose insights into the problems of writing have led to many a more polished product.

# Contents

# Preface

Twenty years ago to say that some one was "chasing ghosts" meant that he was wasting his time in a fruitless flight of folly: pursuing some inane project, such as inventing a perpetual motion machine, or perhaps (on a more practical level, of course) searching for the fountain of youth. Despite the derogatory connotations of the phrase, some people, such as myself, have literally been chasing ghosts as an occupation. What's more, some of us have even caught a few.

Man has long searched for the miraculous or the mysterious. During the Middle Ages the Roman Catholic Church even appointed an investigator to carefully check, verify, or expose the tales of miracles and miraculous acts that were reported to Rome. People who seemed in tune with the miraculous, whether by healing through the laying on of hands, or by levitating their own bodies, or by entering into new vistas of consciousness were often beatified. They were revered by the masses as unique beings in a naïvely conceived world.

Man instinctively likes something that is different. Clothing styles change, modes in science and philosophy constantly evolve, and fads are cultural as well as psychological. Ten years ago astrology columns were read seriously by a few diehards and flippantly by the masses. Today it is a multimillion-dollar business. Belief in witchcraft, which thankfully died out hundreds of years ago, is making a most unwelcome comeback. Cults are blooming, covens are blossoming, and Satanic churches are taking in the harvest. A few hundred years ago to claim to be a witch would entitle the boaster to anything from the stocks to the pyre or to the ax. Today it seems that to claim to be a witch is quite in fashion and considered very suave.

People today are making all sorts of assertions—that they possess ESP, are in contact with space visitors (although this fad has somewhat died down), have a ghost in their house or at least have encountered one or two, speak with the dead, move objects by the mind, are in possession of some secret knowledge, and on and on. And this is where I come in.

For all practical purposes I am a ghost chaser. I check out the claims of these people. But instead of being armed with credulity and superstition, my armory consists of psychology and technology. No one today who has watched the vast cultural revolution can fail to see that the forbidden topics of yesteryear—extrasensory perception (ESP), mind over matter, haunted houses—are gaining a new credibility and scientific respect. Not only are these topics popular, but also such journals as the *Journal of Neuropsychiatry*, as well as magazines such as *Newsweek* and *Nature*, are giving elaborate attention to them. Because of this a few people are turning more and more to the scientific study of these elusive abilities.

My own entrance into the field was in 1967 when I made the decision to study psychic phenomena as a full-time occupation. Now just how does one go about becoming a psychical investigator? There are different roads one can take. Most young parapsychologists take the academic avenue—experimental science and then off to the laboratory. Secure in the world of statistics, computers, and laboratories, one can then study ESP by testing people singly or in masses to see if they can guess symbols on cards or make dice fall on certain faces or combinations. The other avenue is one that is hardly ever traveled. That is the road of the psychical investigator. Now unfortunately this road is also traveled by a great number of bandits. Because of its very nature, parapsychology—the study of these strange abilities and phenomena—attracts both the credulous and the mentally sick, and, worst of all, the misguided pseudointellectuals. There are all too many well-meaning but incompetent people constantly running around in search of the miraculous who are deceived not only by charlatans but by their own incorrigible will to believe. A house with a leaky waterpipe immediately conjures forth a haunting, the schizophrenic deluged by ranting inner voices becomes looked upon as a medium (which is why so many schizophrenics drift into the psychic field where their delusions can be positively reinforced), and a house rocked by an off-coast sonic boom becomes infested by nonphysical beings.

One of the trickiest areas of parapsychology is that of the field investigator—that person who goes out critically and cautiously in search of the paranormal and tries to get to the root of a report of a psychic or haunting. This area is so difficult because one must be aware of how people will willfully fake psychic phenomena, the many normal and anomalous physical phenomena which often pass for psychic phenomena and psychological effects that can smack of pseudo-ESP. It is hard to gauge which is the more difficult problem. Perhaps it is fraud where the investigator and investigatee each try to outwit the other. During parapsychology's infancy and gradual maturation, which ended with J. B. Rhine's introduction of experimental techniques in ESP testing at Duke University in 1930, psychical research was literally a cops-and-robbers affair. A psychic claimed ESP or mind over matter, in rushed the investigators to try to expose the fraud, and round and round they went. If the psychic won, he was declared genuine, and if the investigator won, well . . . No one who enters this field can afford to downplay the amount of deceit he will encounter. Our inherent fault which William James called "the will to believe" is often the greatest pitfall. Parapsychology is one field in which the benefit of the doubt can never be given. Once in a lecture a well-known humanist psychologist said that "fifty percent of the psychics I know cheat some of the time." When the speaker made this remark, I turned to the person sitting next to me and said, "That's not bad, ninety percent of the psychics I know cheat *all* the time." And those are pretty much the odds one encounters in this field.

Just what constitutes a psychical investigator? Despite the well-meaning pseudoscientists and miracle-mongers who gallantly seek out any report of psychic phenomena brandishing occult explanations instead of swords, there are a few who have made a specialty of carefully and scientifically investigating the paranormal. Investigating a haunted house or a medium takes not only a full knowledge of psychical research but several other qualities as well, both scientific and humanistic. Hereward Carrington, a psychical investigator whose active career spanned from 1899 to 1958, was perhaps the most prolific and talented field investigator in history. He is as well an idol of mine whose books first aroused my interest in the field and whose writings ultimately convinced me while still a teen-ager that parapsychology should be my chosen field. Carrington wrote in 1930 what he felt to be the basic qualifications of a psychical investigator: ". . . our ideal investigator must have a thorough knowledge of the literature of the subject, he must have a good grounding in normal and abnormal psychology, in physics, chemistry, biology, photography, and some laboratory experience; he must be a keen observer, a good judge of human nature and its motives; he must be well trained in magic and sleight of hand; he must be shrewd, quick of thought and action, ever on the alert, patient, resourceful, open-minded, tolerant, rapid in his observations and deductions, sympathetic, and have a sense of humor."

If one were to try to personify the ideal psychical investigator today, one could do no better.

As I stated, those entering parapsychology have two choices—either to go into the laboratory or into the field. I have been fortunate in that I have had the opportunity to do both, although my love has always been the challenge and intrigue of field investigation.

These points are raised to warn the reader that psychic phenomena are not apples on a tree, ready to be plucked by any chance explorer into their realm. Psychic phenomena are more like rare minerals that must be searched out but are only seldom found. In writing up these investigations both from the field and the laboratory, I have drawn upon several years of labor. No amount of writing could ever do justice to the amount of chaff which must be winnowed before the grain appears.

I well remember my first introduction to the field. I had read everything I could on psychical research and had even gone to a few séances. The first one had been a typical Spiritualist service in Hollywood. Two women who had heard glowing reports of a certain trance medium had called for me and the three of us had driven into Hollywood. The séance in the converted garage had already begun, but we were admitted into the blackened room and for the next hour I was introduced to two aspects of the psychic field—the low level of the fake mediums and the even lower level of their followers. After a dull hour of platitudes, the sitters compared psychic experiences and chatted sociably, while the medium, I noticed, was busily counting the evening's take. It is no wonder that, as my colleague Raymond Bayless says, the only sentiment most Spiritualist ministers hold is "Let us prey!" I was rather the center of attention, for I was very young, inexperienced, and interested—all in all a bright candidate for conversion, or so the medium's followers thought. Spiritualists usually engage neophytes in a hard-sell campaign that would put most used-car salesmen to shame. But I wasn't in a sociable mood; besides I was out three bucks so I hastily withdrew from the scene.

My interest was scientific, not emotional nor religious. And so, armed with the knowledge of the history of parapsychology but little else, I decided to become more actively involved in the field. During these years of 1966–1969, the American Society for Psychical Research (ASPR) had a branch in Beverly Hills. Later the group became semiautonomous and was changed to an affiliate not a branch of the ASPR, under the name of the Southern California Society for Psychical Research (SCSPR). Every week the group held meetings for testing local psychics, and one evening I was able to attend. The psychic was mildly impressive. She went around the table giving her reading to each of us. Every once in a while she seemed to hit upon something psychically. To one sitter she gave the impression, "You have just bought a new car, it is green," which was correct. To a young man sitting opposite me she said that a relative, an aunt, had come to visit. Again, right on the nose. And to a distinguished note-taking gentleman huddled in a corner of the room she offered, "You are a psychologist and are working on a book." Indeed, the man was a University of California, Los Angeles psychiatrist who was about to publish a book. But these impressions were only occasional hits camouflaged within a great amount of vague and confused material.

These first two exposures to the psychic field introduced me to the double-edged sword that I would encounter so often during the forthcoming years—science and discovery on one hand, deceit and delusion on the other. Actually, the two sometimes intertwine.

Before closing this Preface I would like to introduce another person with whom the reader will become well familiar during the course of this book. No one can jump directly into psychical investigations without knowing the tricks of the trade so to speak. And these tricks can only be learned or imparted by that sacred God, experience. How I learned these tricks and gained that experience are due to my colleague, Raymond Bayless, a well-known psychical investigator for the past twenty years, whom I met in 1967. Raymond Bayless had published many accounts of his psychic adventures, including a book, *The Enigma of the Poltergeist*, which chronicled his firsthand encounters.* Since that time Raymond and

* Raymond Bayless, *The Enigma of the Poltergeist* (Englewood Cliffs, N.J.: Prentice-Hall, 1967).

I have been colleagues, and he has shared in most of the pursuits and experiments and battles that comprise this volume.

This then is the world of psychical research, a world of vast discovery and mystification on one hand, and deceit, con artistry, and self-delusion on the other. It is a schizoid world which can affect anyone who touches its Janus-like face. This book will look both at the genuine and the fraudulent, as well as the often incredible controversies which underlie parapsychology. It is a very behind-the-scenes look at what is going on in parapsychology. Yet, despite its often avalanching problems, psychical research is still, to quote Hereward Carrington, ". . . the Science of the Present Century—the most important work being done in the world today—by far the most important."

D. Scott Rogo

# IN SEARCH OF
# THE UNKNOWN

# 1

# The Search for Psychics

Everyone probably has a bit of ESP, but it is so subtle an ability that we rarely notice that we have it. Some of us may have only rare, spontaneous flashes of ESP while others will show it by outguessing chance on statistical card tests. However there is a third type of psychic individual who has been pursued by psychical investigators since parapsychology's birth—the truly gifted subject. Some people are particularly gifted with ESP. The ability plagues them, they can sometimes induce the ESP faculty, and they can even control it to some extent. There are several psychics whose abilities are so consistent that research with them is easy and fruitful. In fact, psychical research made some of its greatest progress by studying these talented sensitives.

However true psychics are rare. It is not odd for a person to have a few psychic experiences and decide that he or she is psychic. This type of self-delusion is common in the field, so the search for sensitives is a never-ending quest.

Where does one find good psychics? There are several ways to go about the search. Most obviously, one must keep one's ear to the ground, follow every lead, and test everyone who seems to be a likely prospect, or one can make the rounds of professional psychics, either showmen or Spiritualist mediums. Every so often a genuine psychic will emerge.

The best psychic talent I have ever worked with, though, was a happenchance volunteer subject who took part in a mass ESP testing program I was carrying out as director of research for the Southern California Society for Psychical Research. I had dropped into the SCSPR office one day to find a new temporary secretary working there. She was introduced to me as Claudia Adams, and since few people are exempt from my continuous recruiting for experiments, she fell prey to my gentle cajoling.

Actually, the experiment was not meant to be for "gifted subjects" but rather for the average unpsychic subject whom we were testing with a procedure that attempted to find a psi-conducive state of consciousness; that is, a mental and/or environmental state that enhances ESP ability. We know that states of mind slightly altered from our waking activity and more internally directed (such as meditation and hypnosis) are more conducive to the emergence of ESP. For our tests, replicating work done at Maimonides Medical Center, we were inducing a mild altered state of consciousness using a sensory isolation technique, the ganzfeld technique. A subject is placed in a soundproofed room or booth, his ears are plugged, and Ping-Pong ball halves are placed over his eyes. The subject is then directed to stare into a light (preferably red) directly in front of him for about half an hour. This simple technique cuts off the subject's access to normal sensory input, and instead he is immersed in his own thoughts, emotions, and daydreaming since images often form against the homogeneous visual field. While the subject reports his thoughts and mental images over an intercom, at one random point (in another room) we try to influence his imagery by staring at a target picture or a series of pictures. Sometimes the subject's imagery simultaneously reflects the picture the agent is looking at and "sending." Later, the subject is also shown four different pictures and must pick out the one we were sending.

Claudia began as only one of thirty subjects I was using with this technique. She arrived at the UCLA-based laboratory (lent to us for the study by Dr. Thelma Moss of the UCLA Neuropsychiatric Institute) promptly at 6:00 P.M. We chatted and then I took her into the lab's isolation chamber, placed the halved Ping-Pong balls over her eyes, put earphones over her head to plug the source of hearing, and instructed her to describe all her mental imagery for half an hour. Claudia had no idea what the target material was to be. Nor for that matter did I.

Leaving the booth, I sat down by the intercom to record all of what she had to report. Simultaneously my assistant, Chris Shepherd, went to ten sealed envelopes, each containing four viewmaster reels, shuffled a special deck of cards, and on the basis of the results chose one reel in one of the envelopes. He also chose one five-minute period during the thirty-five-minute test as a "sending" period. Several minutes passed, and then Chris inserted the target reel into the 3-D viewmaster and began sending.

The target reel was entitled, *The American Indian*, and Chris started to view the first of seven tableaux through the viewmaster which depicted an Indian woman holding a baby at arm's length. No sooner had Chris begun his viewing when Claudia's voice responded from her totally enclosed booth. "Natives . . . native people. I see a bunch of naked people. Also like a mother with a child in her arms. . . ." At that moment Chris clicked the viewer to scene two, an aerial view of a great forest with a gap in the trees across which two dirt roads met. At that moment Claudia's imagery changed: ". . . a forest with a lot of trees. All the trees seem to be in a line so that it's not like I'm looking down at them, but like I'm going down a line of trees." Chris clicked to the third tableau, a view with a canoe rowed by two Indians as seen from the shore. Again, Claudia's imagery cascaded right along with the change of scene: "A sailboat . . . no sail, it's a plain boat. It's rocking up and down on the waves . . . looking out from land and a boat going by. . . ."

All of these images and scenes lasted but two minutes each, then Claudia lost the image. Usually in the ganzfeld we expect the subject only to latch onto the general theme of the target, but Claudia had given recognizable descriptions of three mini-scenes in a row. This was a startling success.

Most people can comprehend the concept of telepathy, the mind's ability to discern thoughts or emotions contained within another mind. But Claudia had done us one better; she had perceived the target even *before* either Chris or I had viewed it. This discovery was made the next morning when I transcribed Claudia's tapes. As I stated, the tree tableau consisted of a view of a forest obviously taken from an airplane. The forest surrounds an open dirt field crossed by two roads which finally merge. In making a transcript of the tape recording, I discovered that a minute *before* Chris opened the sealed envelope containing the target reel, Claudia reported, "Trees, looking down on trees, a lot, it's a forest land or what. Airplane overlooking forest land. The shadow of the wings on top of the trees as it goes by. A road comes into another road; it's not a cross section, just one road coming into another road. A dirt road." So even before our attempt to influence Claudia telepathically, she had given us a grand display of clairvoyance by describing a picture no one had yet seen and in greater detail than the way she described it later telepathically.

A week later I ran three more tests with her, two using the ganzfeld technique, one without. Each test revealed Claudia's ESP ability, but in a very odd way. For these three tests I arranged four packets, each of which contained four pictures clipped from magazines. One of these packets would serve as the target. Four of these sixteen pictures I had used before. They had been in my desk for three years as they were ones I particularly liked. The others I had picked out only a few weeks before.

For the first ganzfeld I picked out a target packet and an individual picture (randomly, of course), waited ten minutes, and then stared at the picture for ten minutes more. The first target was Mount Rushmore. Claudia's ESP was very vague, although her first impression reported from the booth was a fleeting "feeling of stone." Later on, though, she began reporting vague allusions that probably responded to the target, including, "looking up at columns, like ruins," "arches of stone," and so on. These were very unfocused, and Claudia failed to pick out the Rushmore scene when I presented all four targets to her, so these allusions could have been coincidental.

In the next test Claudia merely sat in the darkened isolation booth without the ganzfeld setting since I wanted to compare her performance to the one when she was utilizing the homogeneous field as an imagery stimulant.

Within seconds Claudia began describing images that compelled my full attention: "A lot of space, I feel, it's of space. Now there's a thing with stars—it's black, with a lot of stars— Blackness— Blackness all around— Blackness with light to it; it's not just dead blackness. There are amoeba-type things, little squiggly things. A planet?—a planet—there's something that looks like Saturn with a lot of rings. Definitely have the feeling of space. Like outer space . . ."

I was disappointed, yet tremendously excited and puzzled, for on opening the target envelope the picture was merely a fine color photograph of two cobras. But what was so provocative is that Claudia had given an almost perfect description of another target picture in one of the envelopes. It was a favorite picture of mine which I had used years before. It was a surrealistic one, an outer-space scene with a dazzling black background illuminated by three small planets revolving on each of three corners of the picture. The center of this eerie panorama shows three manikin-like figures floating and revolving in space. Apparently Claudia had bypassed my target selection to focus in on another, a personal favorite of mine. Now, one could say this is coincidence, but Claudia had described all three elements of the picture—the overpowering black background, the planets, and the figures (amoebas).

Would Claudia consistently bypass the target in order to focus on my personal favorites? This question was answered during the third test period, in which we again used the ganzfeld technique. No sooner had we begun when she focused in on a flower image, describing it in detail. Indeed the target was a magnificent color portrait of a rose. She even aptly described its L-shaped stem. These impressions came before I had opened the envelope, but after I had chosen it. After the test she easily picked it out from the control targets.

However, the flower image merged into another scene. Like the outer-space scene which was my favorite, another of my old pictures is a photograph of Carlsbad Caverns with shimmering stalagmites glittering in the light. I had been struck by this photograph when I first saw it and had cut it out and kept it in my desk even though up until now it had not shown up as a target or even as a control. Claudia, now having discussed her flower image and gotten the target, focused right in on the Carlsbad Caverns scene. She envisioned mineral veins, sparkling rocks, "bright sparkling things—something transparent—stalagmites, frozen drops, icicles—a cave—mineral veins in wall. Underground passages . . ."

Toward the end of the session Claudia started to describe a Peruvian scene complete with Indians and "a lot of blankets." When I sorted out the control prints, right next to the flower target in the packet was an impressionistic print showing a group of South American Indians all holding blankets over their heads. So apparently Claudia was about to hit three different targets.

If one thinks this is coincidence, I might add that up to this point in twelve experiments with other subjects only on two occasions did anyone hit an image representing the target and only on one occasion did someone hit another target in the packet.

Claudia's results reveal a great deal about her ESP. Apparently we do not "send" her anything, but instead she scans by ESP, picking up impressions randomly. However, strong emotional settings or involvement seem to guide and focus her ESP. Thus, in our very first test she was able to focus onto Chris's intense viewing of Indian scenes. However, during my three tests with her, she bypassed the target to concentrate extrasensorily not on the targets I had cut out a few weeks before, but on two out of four pictures to which I had an emotional response—ones I was more familiar with and had kept in my desk for three years. Finally, in our last test, Claudia was able to snatch up the target itself in such detail as even to describe the flower's oddly bent stem, and then, after describing the caverns, gained impressions of another target in the packet. (I had planned a fourth test, but since Claudia had already described two of the four remaining targets, I aborted the concluding run.) This type of "leakage" is not rare. During dream-ESP research carried out at Maimonides Medical Center, the experimenter noted on one occasion that if the agent chose a telepathic target, and also a clairvoyant target (left in the envelope and not opened), the subject's dream bypassed the telepathic target and concentrated and incorporated the theme of the clairvoyant target.

Claudia's ESP ability is amazing, but apparently unfocused. She scans and picks up alternate targets or ones to which I have an emotional response. Our present work with her is in helping her to focus her amazing talent.

However, many psychics have even more unfocused abilities than Claudia, and the case of Audrey Manny will show the difficulties inherent in trying to harness and interpret the ESP gift.

In September 1968 Mrs. Manny wrote to me about her psychic ability. Her claims were not idle boasts since no less a noted parapsychologist than W. G. Roll had shown interest in her ability. Roll is project director of the Psychical Research Foundation (PRF) in Durham, North Carolina, and a cautious and critical investigator. He had written in the Foundation's publication *Theta* that, during object association ("psychometry") and other tests, she showed evidence of paranormal abilities, and that he hoped that further work could be done with her.

Since Roll was working on other projects, Audrey Manny thought that I would be interested in testing her. Mrs. Manny lived in the East and I in Los Angeles and this would be unwieldy, but I was determined to try. Her abilities centered on psychometry, where one receives impressions from objects held in the hand such as a watch or wallet. I decided on a long-distance experiment, so I procured from Raymond Bayless an object about which I knew nothing. It was simply a credit card with a meaningless name on it. Thus the experiment was "blind" inasmuch as I could not verify Mrs. Manny's impressions about the object until consulting with Raymond Bayless to check the details. I mailed the card to her and a few days later she phoned me to give her impressions.

Before I give the results, let me tell the story behind the card as I got it from Raymond afterward. The card belonged to a young police officer who had had some dealings with narcotics investigations. He had gone on a fishing trip and had fallen overboard and drowned. However his widow felt sure he had been murdered but her suspicions could never be proved.

With this history in mind we can now evaluate Mrs. Manny's reading. The first thing she told me was that the owner of the card was orphaned and she got the impression of fear and pain. Unfortunately we were not able to verify the first impression, but her second one was fitting, even if vague. She told me that the owner of the card "was fairly young, under thirty, reddish-blond hair, 5'10" to 6'2". All this was fitting except we could not verify the hair color. Her third major impression was directly on the target. Mrs. Manny said that the man was dead, had died painfully, and she got a feeling of pain in her chest. Drowning is a painful experience and does entail chest pain. I might also add that this was the only time when a subject specifically said the card's owner was dead in the several times I have used this object for test purposes. Her next impression was off the mark but curiously had an element of accuracy. She said that he was a soldier and may have died aboard the *Pueblo*. Now at first glance this may seem a flat "miss." However, Mrs. Manny qualified her statement by saying that the soldier impression was based on her vision of the target being in uniform. This is a problem one often runs into while studying a psychic. Her impression was correct—a man in uniform. Her interpretation—he was a soldier—was wrong. This type of interference by the psychic's own rational mind is one of the commonest sources of error that blocks a successful psychic reading. Her *Pueblo* impression also is both correct and incorrect. He certainly had been aboard a boat, but not the *Pueblo*, of course. Here again Mrs. Manny most likely received a correct impression but her mind, either consciously or unconsciously, translated the image of death and a boat into a more rational association with the "man in uniform" impression. The whole thought process would go something like this: "I see a man in uniform killed in a boat, so he must be a soldier or in the military, thus he died aboard the *Pueblo*." Luckily Mrs. Manny qualified her soldier impression as being her own rationalization. Had she stuck with her simple, uninterpreted impressions, her reading probably would have been more accurate. But instead her own mind added a complicating factor.

Later that evening, as Mrs. Manny told me, she tried for more impressions. Again she got the themes of fear and pain. But this time she got more: he might have been on narcotics. Again the theme is correct—narcotics—but not the interpretation. She repeated her *Pueblo* impression and ended by saying that the subject had left behind a wife and child. True enough, but not beyond being a logical deduction from the fact she believed the man dead.

Nonetheless, Audrey's reading was good, in fact very good, and certainly worth more research. Already her psychic talent revealed several things to me, most notably that it was vague and not totally reliable, and secondly she had an overactive unconscious that often infiltrated and distorted her impressions. This type of distortion has been noted by every psychic and every investigator in the past, so this factor was no revelation. But great psychics seem to be able to overcome this to some degree. Mrs. Manny had yet to develop to that level.

In order to offset this problem I began a series of long-distance precognition tests with standard ESP cards (Zener cards). Mrs. Manny would try to guess beforehand the order of the cards, a series of twenty-five, printed with either a star, cross, wavy lines, square, or circle. There might be some objection that this type of testing was pretty shallow, since Audrey's abilities were basically qualitative not quantitative. However it was Audrey who had told me that she had been very successful with this type of test and inasmuch as she liked doing the card tests and since a firm statistical appraisal could be made from them, why not? Unfortunately her enthusiasm was not matched by her psychic ability which failed to function on the card tests we ran. She never scored above the chance score of approximately five hits per twenty-five.

The psychology of Audrey's ESP had two elements. First, her ability to focus in on something psychically and spontaneously exhibit ESP. Second was her own subconscious that could often trick her into ascribing supernormal abilities to unconscious processes. For example, she had developed the talent for automatic writing, wherein she would make herself passive, take pen or pencil in her hand, and begin to write unconsciously. Sometimes ESP-based information would be written out. During her writings she began a series of Chinese communications. Rows and rows of Chinese characters were written out and Audrey was sure this writing was beyond anything within her own mind. However she did admit that she had casually studied Chinese twenty years before. She sent these scripts to me and I in turn took them to the Oriental Language Department at UCLA. My suspicions were confirmed. The writings were merely Chinese strokes and pseudo-Chinese characters mixed together in a meaningless hodgepodge. Automatic writing, like the Ouija board, is an open sesame to the subconscious, and Audrey's unconscious familiarity with Chinese characters had used the writing to emerge into consciousness.

This type of "communication" is not rare with psychics. Minnie Soule and Helene Smith, two psychics of yesteryear, came up with Martian languages. Professor Theodore Flournoy, Mlle Smith's investigator, took great pains to show how her Martian language, while bizarre to the eye, followed the grammatical structure of the French language. Mlle Smith also wrote a few phrases of Sanskrit which were presumably picked up subconsciously during her extensive reading.

Despite the setbacks in the formal research with Audrey, her flashes of ESP were striking enough that they could be verified. When I was in the East during the summer of 1969, Mrs. Manny told me over the phone that she had the sudden impression that someone very close to her was about to die. Within a day, news came that a close friend of her mother-in-law had died. (Audrey was a widow.) Luckily there was a witness to the impression, her fiancé, and I was able to get a statement from him verifying the entire incident.

Mrs. Manny's romantic involvement was taking precedence over her psychic work, so my explorations into her abilities began a downhill trek. We spoke occasionally over the phone when she had something psychic to report, but this gradually diminished also.

Not all leads are as successful as the Adams or even the Manny cases. Usually one finds nothing but the worst hokum. Raymond Bayless and I had heard great claims about an alleged psychic holding forth south of Los Angeles. So we drove down to have a look. The address we had turned out to be a store with the odd sign "Artists' Supplies—Lessons—Séances." We walked in to find that the front of the store opened into a sitting area which had been converted into a chapel. A huge birdcage was in one corner of the sitting area and pretty, bright-colored tropical birds were flying freely throughout the room. The medium turned out to be an old-fashioned "billet reader." This entails writing down a question on a piece of paper and sealing it. The medium then holds it to her forehead and gives her "psychic" impressions, allegedly repeating the sealed message without opening the billet and giving a psychic answer to any query contained therein. There are many ways to fake billet reading, and this practitioner used the oldest and most unoriginal of them all. The trick is absurdly simple. All the billets are collected from the guests and handed over to the medium who selects one, gains her "psychic" impressions from it, and then opens it to read to the audience. Then a little speech is given stating that at the first writer's request no names or initials would be used and everything would remain anonymous. Actually this "reading" is a dummy one and applies to no one in the room, but she does open one of the guest's billets and memorizes its contents. Now she picks up another billet but actually answers the question written on the first billet and offers the writer's name or initials which are usually also scribbled on the paper. This makes it appear as though she is psychically picking up information from the envelope in her hand while really she is merely repeating what she read on the previous billet. This second billet is then duly opened and memorized and the whole procedure is repeated on and on. In effect the medium keeps reading one ahead of herself.

If there is anything worse than a con artist, it's an incompetent con artist. And this doyenne of the psychic arts certainly was. She had a horrible memory and kept giving the wrong messages to the wrong billet. It was comical. To highlight the evening, as the gentle chords of the chapel organ rolled forth, two of the colorful little birds (which by the way had apparently been trained to chirp gleefully when the organ music began) decided to engage in a free-for-all. One dive-bombed the other, screeching raucously. Neither was hurt, but the ensuing chirps-of-war and scattered feathers made a hilarious sight. It was a fitting denouement to an absurd evening.

Actually any sort of psychic stunt where either a written message or a blindfold is used is bound to be a trick. David Abbott in his handbook on fraudulent psychic tricks, *Behind the Scenes with the Mediums*, lists thirty different classifications of billet illusions. Showmen like Kreskin, David Hoy, Dunninger take advantage of the public's lack of expertise in the art of mentalism by using these same worn-out tricks, leading the audience to wonder if it really was a trick or ESP. As W. E. Cox, a magician-turned-parapsychologist has said, "An audience usually is left to wonder how best to classify them; and therein lies the greatest of their deceptions." ("Parapsychology and Magicians," *Parapsychology Review*, May–June 1974.)

However one cannot merely dismiss stage performers who masquerade as psychics as worthless. For some may actually have a glimmer of ESP ability which originally led them into stage performances. In *From Anecdote to Experiment in Psychical Research*, the revered parapsychologist R. H. Thouless wrote that, since the psychical investigator is "always looking out for gifted subjects, the variety stage might be a good direction in which to look."*

Most stage performers use a variety of tricks for mind-reading acts—codes, hidden microphones, and countless others. While these tricks are well known, certain famous stage telepathists and mind-reading teams have convinced some parapsychologists that they possess some ESP ability.

All this merely goes to prove the point that the search for good ESP subjects leads one in many directions, even to professional psychics and stage performers. Most are fakes, pure and simple, but every so often something startling happens as the following anecdote illustrates.

One afternoon Raymond and I were thinking of making the rounds of some local professional psychics. For many years there had been a woman holding forth in the Los Angeles area who advertised herself in the Yellow Pages of the telephone directory as "The Mystery Woman of Radio Fame." The ad further read that she had been a performer with Robert Ripley's "Believe it or Not" show and offered "spiritual counseling" which is a euphemism for giving psychic readings. Since by county ordinance professional fortune-telling and other occult practices are prohibited in Los Angeles, professional psychics do have to use discretion in how they advertise and operate. This is done either by hiding behind religion by getting easily available ordinations, or by only requiring "love offerings" (and note the word *requiring*), or holding themselves out as spiritual counselors.

We phoned the "Mystery Woman" and Raymond made an appointment for us under assumed names for the next day. The retired stage performer really had unmistakable ESP ability. She asked Raymond to tap on her hand the number of letters in a name he was thinking of. Raymond tapped four times and gradually after some hesitation she said, "Emma," which was correct. She gave Raymond some other impressions which were also correct. Her

* R. H. Thouless, *From Anecdote to Experiment in Psychical Research* (London: Routledge and Kegan Paul, 1972).

reading for me was brief but accurate. She asked me to tap out my first name on her hand since I had come completely anonymously. Actually I go by my middle name and have never used my first name, only the initial. Nevertheless I tapped out seven letters. The psychic correctly said, "I think there is an O and an A in the name. . . . Wait. . . . Something is wrong. You don't go by your first name but by a nickname or something." The psychic then said I had tried to trick her and refused to go on with the reading at all. I tried to offer her the two-dollar fee she usually charged, but our mystery woman seemed honest, a rarity among professional psychics, and said, "You didn't get no spiritual counseling."

After the sitting we chatted with the psychic, telling her that we would like to carry out some formal tests with her. Surprisingly she was very cooperative, but since her husband was in the hospital she couldn't give up the time from her professional readings. She did however offer us her services when the crisis was over. Unfortunately that never came to pass; her husband's illness persisted and our very promising subject drifted away from us.

I must admit though that the mystery lady was the only honest and genuine theatrical psychic I have ever encountered. The others have either been self-deluded, crooked, or an odd mixture of both.

I was checking a stage psychic in San Diego who was holding forth weekly in a little auditorium downtown. I walked in and immediately an elderly gentleman walked up to me and engaged me in some casual conversation. He seemed inappropriately interested in my personal life and it didn't take much deduction to figure out that he was the psychic's confederate. So I gave him some perfectly absurd information. The demonstration was ready to begin. First we had a little *moment musicale* and had to sit through the damnedest perversion of the "Moonlight Sonata" I'd ever heard. The "psychic" made a regal entry and began her readings. When she came to me, she merely gushed forth the same nonsense I had given her aide. I cheerfully denied everything much to the performer's consternation.

If one is searching purely for evidence of ESP, instances such as

the genuine encounters narrated previously are striking and convincing. But that is where they stop. Certainly, Mrs. Manny and
the mystery woman had proved their ESP abilities. But psychical
research is more than just proving or gathering evidence for ESP.
It is a quest to understand the nature of extrasensory communication, the laws or principles which govern it, how it can be
developed and used. From this standpoint, the work with Mrs.
Manny was a loss. So too are most occasions when one merely tries
to verify someone's psychic talents. Once I had a sitting with the
well-known English psychic, Doris Collins, during which she did
hit upon a few things pertinent to my private life. But, so what? I
certainly didn't need to go to a medium to be told these things.
The British cynic, Dennis Bradley, once remarked that the trouble
with psychic readers was that he got sick of hearing about himself.
The real purpose behind psychical exploration is not only the discovery of gifted psychics, but also procuring their services for a
research project. Only in this way can discoveries about ESP and
the psychic personality be made.

My first chance to work with a gifted subject came in December
1968. At that time UCLA was developing a program of experimental courses. These courses were extracurricular, but students
could petition the heads of their departments for credit in taking
them. Starting in 1967 a course in parapsychology had been offered
and in 1968 I undertook to coordinate it for the academic year
1968–1969.

During this period many leads came in, most of them dead ends.
When people think they are psychic or have a ghost in their home,
they invariably call any local University. Most of the public is
under the grave misconception that parapsychology is fully in-
tegrated within the academic scene. This is definitely not the case.
During the 1970s there has been a greater acceptance of parapsychology on the college campus and many courses have started
to spring up. But the climax to the growing academic respectability
and acceptance of parapsychology really only came in 1974 when,

under the sponsorship of the Parapsychology Foundation, an educational and grant-giving organization in New York, the University of California, Santa Barbara announced the creation of a full-time lectureship in the subject for 1974–1975. However, the academic breakthrough is still a long uphill battle, and generally when calls on psychic matters come into a university, odds are that the institution will have no one competent to handle them. The situation in 1968 was even worse. However, calls to UCLA usually went to one of two places: either to Dr. Thelma Moss at the Neuropsychiatric Institute or to me.

One call I received was from Richard Carl Spurney, a philosophy instructor at Long Beach City College. Spurney wanted me to take part in some experiments in which he was engaged with several gifted subjects. He really didn't have to introduce himself to me as I already knew of him and was familiar with the work he was doing. Spurney had found a gifted psychic, Joyce Partise, and was accumulating evidence of her ESP abilities. He had already taken her to the UCLA Neuropsychiatric Institute, and she had impressed Dr. Moss. Local newspapers such as the *Los Angeles Times* had carried stories on Spurney and Mrs. Partise and even magazine articles were starting to appear. Dick was new to the field, but he was making a valiant attempt at studying a difficult aspect of psychical research. The crux of the work was not, "Do my subjects have ESP?"—that was already well established—but was on one aspect of psychometry that had been baffling researchers for decades. Why was it that some people could go to a psychic and get splendid results, while someone else would experiment with the same sensitive and get nothing? I had seen this with Raymond on a few occasions. He would get good results with a subject but I would get zero. Even in experimental parapsychology this principle was known and was dubbed the "experimenter effect." Some parapsychologists would get splendid results in their ESP projects while others could never seem to run a successful experiment. It had long been accepted that only investigators with certain personality traits could experiment in such a way as to keep their subjects so at ease and comfortable that their ESP abilities could manifest unhampered. Uncomfortable physical or psychological conditions might easily block ESP.

This theory was pretty vague. What are these elusive qualities of the good experimenter or sitter? This was the question that Dick had in mind as he watched Mrs. Partise work, and it was this question that was occupying his thoughts when he called me. At the time Dick was working with another sensitive, Anne Soyka, and it was with Anne that I saw a first-rate psychometrist in action. Anne was a pretty young housewife in her early thirties. She had a knockout figure, dark hair, an outgoing personality, and unending cooperativeness when it came to demonstrating her abilities. She was a friend of Joyce Partise and it was through her that Anne met and formed a working alliance with Spurney.

Watching Anne work was a marvelous experience. There was no tempermentalism, no vagueness or fishing for information during her psychic readings. She merely picked up an object, handled it for a few seconds, and then started to reel off a series of impressions about its owner. During these tests Anne sat with Dick, myself, and a few others in a partitioned-off room. The owners of the day's bevy of objects were placed in another room. Anne never saw her sitters before the sitting. During my first series of tests with her, Dick handed her a plain gold band as the token object. She fingered it for a few moments, closed her eyes, and then began an incredible list of impressions: the owner was male, he had played on the football team in high school, he traveled a lot and had lived in nine different cities of the United States, had recently received a draft deferment on religious grounds, his eyebrows met over the bridge of his nose, and so forth. After the reading Dick drew a rough map of the United States and handed it to Anne, asking her to note where the sitter had lived. She drew a large egg-shaped form on the map saying that it was in this general area.

After the reading was completed the subject was allowed to enter. He was a husky ex-high-school football player who was one of Dick's students. We went over the list of impressions and one by one Carl (as I'll call him) verified each one. He had lived in precisely nine different cities, and upon listing them we found that they all were very much within the oval Anne had drawn. It was, and still is, the most amazing psychic reading I had ever seen. There was one hang-up though. Carl's eyebrows obviously did not meet and join together. Carl smirked as he admitted that his eyebrows did join together but he shaved between them to separate them.

We were due to begin another test so I slipped Anne an object of my own. I was curious to see what she would get because I seldom get very good results with psychics. I am afraid my ice-cold disposition during my investigations is not congenial, and my poker face during the scoring and experimenting with Anne was a standing joke between Dick and myself. Anne did not know whose object she held. Then came her impressions: the object's owner liked to cook, preferred small women, loved tapioca pudding, and owned a unicycle. All wrong! However it seemed likely that a bit of displacement was going on. This is a principle well known with gifted subjects that Spurney did not know about and so had subsequently overlooked. If a psychic is reading for an exceptionally good sitter and then another sitter is introduced, she may go right on reading for the original sitter. Anne's impressions about my object were completely wrong, irrefutably and incontestably wrong. But my reading had come right after Carl's, so I called him back again and one by one went over these impressions with him. Yes, he liked to cook and his girl friends were always small. Tapioca pudding was his favorite dessert and he had an absolute fetish about it. He did own a unicycle. I doubt if anyone by pure guesswork or by chance could have hit upon the fact that a sitter liked tapioca pudding *and* owned a unicycle. The accuracy of these unusual impressions about Carl substantiated the displacement theory and added a new dimension in the work with Anne.

As I said, displacement is not a rare phenomenon, and the history of gifted subjects is riddled with it. Eugene Osty, the pioneering French physician, found that psychics pick up impressions not necessarily only about the owner of an object but even about people who had merely peripherally come in contact with it. During tests with the great American medium, Mrs. Leonore Piper, if two séances were held on the same day, impressions and communications during the second séance might still be directed to the sitters who participated in the first. During psychometry experiments with Mrs. Warren Elliot, H. F. Saltmarsh found that before she could zero in on an object's owner she often gave impressions about the Society for Psychical Research office, where the objects had been collected, or its secretary who had cataloged them. Even in conventional ESP testing it became evident that subjects might consistently guess correctly either one before or one after the Zener card being concentrated upon.

By gradually sifting out good and bad sitters, Dick had tried to isolate what traits made up the successful sitter. This had led him to develop a questionnaire asking such things as social views, attitudes, and so forth, based upon the information his psychics had imparted to him about who they liked to read for. My second series of experiments, predominantly with Anne, was to test the efficiency of this. Dick had collected a crew of high- and low-scoring subjects by the use of the questionnaire, and one by one the objects they donated were given to Anne. We tried to judge accuracy and length of the readings offered. Sure enough those high-scoring agents got long and generally accurate readings. (When Anne was hot she was 75 to 80 percent accurate.) The low-scoring subjects got vague, confused, and short readings. Actually Anne had a good track record of her own in predicting whether the object she touched belonged to either a high or low scorer.

Spurney was convinced his test had been validated, but I was less sure for two reasons. First was a relatively minor point. In my opinion his method of scoring the readings was too subjective and qualitative, so I showed him a more objective mathematical method of appraising the scoring. My second argument was that Spurney had never taken into account the displacement factor, and I felt that in many instances readings were bad as mine had been because the impressions might really be applicable to the previous sitter.

Despite these two reservations there was an odd and inexplicable pattern of success and failure correlated with scorings on the questionnaire. To Spurney it was the questionnaire that counted. To me, it was the psychological principles behind it. Who then makes a good sitter? If anyone were to try to make a psychological appraisal of Spurney's questionnaire, he would probably be consternated. It had no form, many questions seemed nonsensical, and the whole test was vague. But this is not Spurney's fault since he is not a psychologist. He was basing the form on what his psychics told him were positive traits for sitters. From a psychological standpoint this is what can be said about the successful experimenter or sitter which the questionnaire echoes: he is extroverted; unneurotic and nonego centered; he likes people, is very sensitive to people about him; and is conscientious. These few basic traits seemed linked for success with a psychic. Perhaps in the future psychologists can take some of Spurney's "good sitters" or discover new ones with other first-rate psychics and then carry out psychological evaluations. (For example, I never saw Carl get a bad sitting.)

While I saw Anne on several occasions I only saw Joyce Partise once. Dick had worked out a testing session with her and asked me to attend. He later had to cancel the meeting but forgot to call me. So on the scheduled night Raymond, who had not taken part in the work with Anne at all, Joyce Vera, a friend of mine who often went with me on local investigative expeditions, and I drove to the home of Mr. and Mrs. Partise, only to find a very startled couple. They understood the difficulty and were hospitable and apologetic. Mrs. Partise gave both Raymond and me readings but mine was pretty well a blank. However she did tell Raymond that his father had worked in a shoe factory as a young man and that the Maltese cross had special significance to him (Raymond). These were correct impressions.

I had hoped to carry out independent work with Anne separately from Dick's and he was all for it. Anne had devoted herself willingly to long hours of service, never accepting a penny for her work. But this was an age of theatrics and the show business circuit was a temptation. Peter Hurkos, the stage psychic, was going strong, and even Joyce Partise had done television spots. Any hope of further research was deadened by Anne's determination to go show biz. Teaming up with Joyce Partise they dubbed themselves "the psychic twins" and attempted to make a go of it on local television. Unfortunately neither of them had the necessary flair for this type of exposure, nor the consistency of their ESP, to be a full-blown success at this endeavor. The last I saw of Anne was just a few months after the experiments with Dick. She phoned me to say she was going on "Tempo," wanted a bit of information from me, and asked if she could use my name as having worked with her. I gave my O.K. and watched her appearance the next day. She was able to give the talk show host a fairly decent reading when she held a token of his and got the impressions of a crash in which three men had died. The host's token had belonged to a friend of his who had been killed along with two fellow soldiers in a helicopter crash in Vietnam.

Shortly after this appearance Anne, her husband, and family moved to Denver where her husband had been transferred.

By now the question arises, just how can one tell whether or not a subject is really just "lucky" and gets a few details by pure coincidence mixed in with a lot of vague impressions? It was this question that led parapsychologists to work out ways of judging if a psychic does have a definable ESP ability or whether we are just misinterpreting lucky guesswork. This is especially true when one is working with a psychic whose ability is vague. If a psychic gives one good hit, but then several wrong impressions, it is nearly impossible to judge whether ESP or a lucky guess was at work. A series of tests that show how this difficulty can be surmounted was carried out in 1974 with a nurse, Mrs. Helen Niesen, who felt she had psychic ability. The tests were conducted by Raymond Bayless and myself.

Mrs. Niesen, a nonprofessional psychic, liked to gain impressions from photographs. So for the experiment I gave her two snapshots and after staring at them she reeled off about twenty-seven impressions for each. From a qualitative angle, her readings were good—for Subject A (R.N.) she correctly stated that the man had written plays and appeared in them, that he worked with five people, and that he may have been a good lawyer (the subject had planned a law career but had turned from it during his college days). These few "hits" were interspersed with a lot of vague impressions.

To test if Mrs. Niesen really was demonstrating ESP, I typed out a statement-by-statement summary of her readings and scaled each impression on a 1 to 5 point gauge (5 being very characteristic of the subject, 4 being characteristic, 3 being vague and general but applicable, 2 being general and not applicable, 1 being a "miss.") I then scored the readings as they pertained to *me* and came up with a score of 58 points. Then I gave the reading to R.N. and two control subjects. I told them that this reading was meant for one of them, but did not tell them for which one. Each of them was to score the reading as though pertaining to himself. The two controls gave it scores of 62 and 67. However R.N. himself scored it at 77 points, significantly above what I or the two controls had scored it. This indicates that the reading was particularly directed toward R.N. for whom it was meant, and this indicated ESP. Had no ESP mediated Mrs. Niesen's reading it is highly unlikely that R.N. would have scored it higher than the rest of us.

The second photograph belonged to a friend of mine, J.H. Again Mrs. Niesen got some direct hits, including his intense dislike for doctors, that he uses his fingers in his work (he teaches massage), and most notably that he drove a car that was not his own and that the car was red. J.H., when in Los Angeles, drives a car belonging to a co-worker, a bright red Volkswagen. Using the same method as above, J.H. scored the reading with 77 points while the controls gave scorings of 60, 62, and 65.

The ESP ability is capricious at best. Two weeks later I tested Mrs. Niesen again. She gave five readings on five photographs. I gave all five records to each of the subjects who donated snapshots, instructing them to pick out the one reading that each thought applied to himself. None of them could.

The ESP ability takes strange forms and one of the most intriguing is the rather unusual ability of a subject working with Dr. Thelma Moss. Luckily I was able to take part in these experiments after they were already in progress. Mary Wimberley was totally blind; one eye was glass, the other had had its optic nerve severed. A young woman in her late twenties, Mary had been impressed by Soviet experiments where subjects had been able to guess colors they touched while blindfolded or in a totally dark room. An intelligent woman who, despite her handicap, had earned a master's degree in Russian, she resolved to develop a similar ability. She had had no experience with "skin vision" but was willing to spend several hours a day trying to develop the talent, and she approached Dr. Moss, who agreed to become her most unusual mentor. Together they spent considerable weeks trying to sensitize Mary's fingers to different colors. Mary was soon able to distinguish color by touch. This, in itself, had little to do with ESP, but during the experiments she did show a moderate and fairly consistent ESP ability. Dr. Moss made her first presentation on Mary at the convention of the Parapsychological Association in Edinburgh during September 1972. In her paper Dr. Moss showed that over several trials Mary could successfully distinguish colors by merely handling objects no matter what the material was. Further, she could also distinguish colors even if the targets were placed inside a plastic folder. This would rule out the possibility that somehow she "read" by the texture of the object. This was also ruled out by many impromptu tests in which I would challenge Mary by using objects of odd materials which she could never have been exposed to before. She was very often successful. After one series of tests Dr. Moss and I just started handing her all sorts of different objects and Mary had six hits in a row calling a variety of colors. The very first time we ever used colored tissue paper, she started calling an amazing sequence of correct answers. Moss had also carried out ESP tests in which she had to guess the color of the object the experimenter was thinking of. While not so successful as her dermooptic sense, Mary's ESP seemed definite. At the convention Dr. Moss presented Mary herself. In the demonstration that followed, a volunteer parapsychologist (K. Ramakrishna Rao) handed her random pieces of either black or white crepe paper. Mary hit 100 percent in discriminating between the two. This was impressive at the time, but later at UCLA I thought I could feel a slight difference of texture between the two colored papers. I had myself blindfolded and on my first try could hit 100 percent in differentiating between a stack of ten random black and white pieces. (And no, I didn't read down my nose!) However, at the Edinburgh convention Mary was also given a series of colored plastic pens which would not have been texturally different. Again she was amazingly accurate.

When we returned to Los Angeles, I started experimenting with Mary once a week at the Neuropsychiatric Institute along with Dr. Moss and Christa Lubke, a psychology student from the University of Freiburg. This research was much more tightly controlled than the original work with Mary. In the first experiments Mary knew what four or five colors were being used and was given immediate feedback; that is, told if she were right or wrong on each call. Since the order of the colors was usually chosen haphazardly and spontaneously by Dr. Moss, this could have caused two problems: (1) Was Mary second-guessing Moss's choices or (2) did Dr. Moss consistently choose one color more often than any other which happened to match a calling preference by Mary? For example, during a four-color discrimination test Dr. Moss might choose the color blue more often than any other. If she did and Mary happened to guess blue more often than any other color just by habit, the results would be spurious.

Now let me say emphatically that the consistency of Mary's abilities outweighs either of these two objections. Dr. Moss was not really testing Mary experimentally. The entire research period had hitherto been one of training and development of dermo-optic per-ception, not of rigid experimental research.

But now it was time for some hard-core experimentation. The first change of procedure was the use of totally random sequences of colored objects. Using this technique we ran three different types of tests: dermo-optic perception; "sensing," in which Mary would only hold the colored object on a clipboard and move it close to her skin; and ESP tests with the same colors. After completing several of these tests, a clear pattern became obvious. Although Mary was successful on all three tasks, she consistently scored best on the dermo-optic tests, followed by sensing and finally lowest at ESP. But even so her ESP scores were well over statistical signifi-cance which is gauged to be 100 to 1 odds against chance.

My own interest was of course the ESP tests, and Mary was very eager to pursue them. Usually the ESP tests were run with Mary in the lab and the sender (myself) either downstairs in Dr. Moss's office or in an isolation booth in the lab. Some of the tests were GESP runs (general extrasensory perception). This means ei-ther telepathy or clairvoyance could have been employed, with Mary either picking up the response from my mind or by directly perceiving the color of the target. Other tests were given for PC (pure clairvoyance), and in these tests the agent was in a totally dark room so that the colors could not be distinguished at all. For the target material we would use colored paper, and Mary could guess well above chance which of four or five colors we were con-centrating upon. However, Mary showed another feature common among good ESP subjects—experimenter effects. She consistently worked better with some agents than with others. We alternated among myself, Christa Lubke, and Miss Saba, one of Dr. Moss's assistants. I seemed to get the best results, then Miss Saba and then Miss Lubke. Mary also revealed a tendency for focusing on a cer-tain color during an ESP run. Once, although she was only scoring at chance level, every time blue was the target color she would call it successfully. This lasted throughout an entire experimental run.

My interest in the dermo-optic perception was relatively minor but I did develop a new type of test for it. Hitherto Mary had been discriminating between colors of the same material—differentiating colors of plastic cups, paper, fabric, and so forth. Could Mary, if given a large number of different types of objects, isolate them into different stacks of the same colors? So we gave her a tray full of red, green, and yellow cups, paper, and fabric. Indeed, Mary could make the distinction with obvious ease and could sort them into separate piles based on their color.

It could not be by coincidence that Mary was so gifted with both ESP and some form of subliminal perception. Could there be a connection between the abilities? This seems likely in Mary's case at least. Subliminal perception (SP) is a phenomenon known to psychology in which a subject responds to a signal that is below the threshold of consciousness. A good example would be the "Pötzl phenomenon" in which a subject is shown a picture briefly via a tachistoscope, too briefly in fact for the viewer to retain a full memory of it. Otto Pötzl discovered that elements of the picture, while lost to the consciousness, had been subliminally or unconsciously perceived, and would appear during subsequent dreaming.

Mary's abilities drew upon this same type of phenomenon. Upon touching color she had trained herself to respond automatically. In that way she could "guess" intuitively at the color she was touching. (On occasions, though, the process would become a conscious one.) At this point Mary was responding to a below-the-conscious-level signal. Now in the "sensing" tests this subliminal perception signal was even weaker, and when we removed the signal altogether, her ESP compensated for it. It would be like a radio that continued to play after it had been turned off. Mary's consistent continuum from skin vision to ESP holds great promise in the possibility of training subjects in ESP. It shows that when a subject has been trained to respond by subliminal perception, ESP can take over when the signal is withdrawn. ESP is an incredibly elusive faculty. Subliminal perception is also elusive but it is *still* physical perception. Perhaps the best way to approach ESP is by way of subliminal perception. Perhaps Mary's own ESP abilities only developed because of her self-training in recognizing very weak perceptual messages. A few parapsychologists have already broken ground in this area and their research has been fruitful. (Martin Johnson in Holland and Drs. Hans and Shulamith Kreitler of Tel Aviv have carried out SP-ESP tests. In the Kreitler experiments it was found that the best ESP results were obtained when the ESP signal contradicted a SP message. A long-range implication of this finding could be that the two faculties might work together monitoring each other.)

How does Mary perceive the colors of objects that she holds? It is not solely a learning function since she can respond correctly to new material immediately. On the other hand she is usually not responding to texture—although crepe paper of different colors does have different surface textures which Mary probably does read since even nongifted subjects such as myself can do it. Reading colors through plastic sheets outlaws several physical explanations even though this procedure does dull her accuracy. Experiments in a totally darkened room have been successfully undertaken, so this rules out the possibility that she is somehow responding to heat absorption due to light on the colors.

Mary's dermo-optic perception does manifest surprisingly like ESP—to such an extent it is tempting to postulate that ESP might be part of her subliminal perception process. For example, during long experimentation Mary's abilities decline in accuracy. This is similar to ESP scoring which also declines as the experiment progresses. Secondly there is a principle in parapsychology called "the observer effect" which occurs when a new person is introduced into an experiment and ESP often goes into retreat until the subject becomes used to or comfortable with the individual. While not a distinguishing feature of Mary's abilities, I have seen this effect on several occasions.

However Mary's dermo-optic perception is not ESP, nor do I believe that ESP is even that great an implicating factor. If it were, she should have responded on our ESP tests just as well as she did on the color perception tests, which she did not. Furthermore, her

ESP ability is not nearly as accurate nor as precise as her color perception. In fact, sometimes her fingertip perception is more accurate than ESP has ever been shown to be.

Clearly Mary is an enigma and much more work is needed to get to the root of her abilities. Mary is herself philosophical about it and is now freely devoting her time to teaching color discrimination to young blind children as she herself learned it on her own and with Dr. Moss. Here appreciation certainly should be given to the Parapsychology Foundation which provided a large grant to further research with Mary in 1972.

The Wimberley case also tells us a bit about the nature of some critics of parapsychology. Attending the Edinburgh conference was Professor C. E. M. Hansel, one of parapsychology's most verbal critics and author of a critical but very inaccurate book on ESP.* I challenged him to test Mary for himself after checking it out with Dr. Moss and Mary, and he agreed. A test was arranged for the next day but Hansel never showed up nor has he ever explained why.

The search for psychic subjects takes a most diversified path. One never knows exactly what to expect. Mary Wimberley and Anne Soyka had entirely different gifts of ESP which manifested in totally different ways. Yet each has a talent which represents an aspect of a primary ability that we all most likely possess to some degree. Why did these two talented individuals develop ESP? What subtle psychological characteristic lead them to gain control over a faculty that in most of us occurs sporadically at best? And why in such different forms? These are questions that can only be answered by well-thought-out research with gifted subjects. It is also the reason for a continuing search for psychics.

* C. E. M. Hansel, *ESP: A Scientific Evaluation* (New York: Scribner's, 1966).

# 2

# Experiments with Blue Harary

The psychic talent is a varied one. Some people like Mary Wimberley seem only able to use their ESP to discriminate card symbols or colors. Others, like Mrs. Niesen or Anne Soyka, gain intuitive flashes of information, sometimes detailed, about people or about objects they hold. Still others, Claudia Adams, for example, can conjure up mental images corresponding to pictures in sealed envelopes.

Everyone in parapsychology eagerly listens to the grapevine for news of the latest star subjects, and in 1973 ear-stretching reports began coming out of North Carolina about a subject, Stuart "Blue" Harary, who could "project his mind" away from his body and perceive distant scenes and report correctly on them. With some help from a Parapsychology Foundation grant and the promise of a consultantship at the Psychical Research Foundation I was able to spend six weeks working with Blue Harary.

Durham! If there is any word that is magic in parapsychology, it is the name of this rural, tobacco-processing North Carolina city. As a city it hasn't much to say for itself. It is small, overindustrialized, and dank. Yet, it was here at Duke University that modern parapsychology was born. It was here that J. B. Rhine began his ESP experiments and scientifically proved its existence. It was here that "mind over matter" was also demonstrated experimentally. And it is still today the parapsychological capital of the world. Two of the leading United States parapsychology organizations were founded in Durham. When Rhine retired from Duke, the university's parapsychology laboratory followed him off campus and became the Institute for Parapsychology of the Foundation for Research on the Nature of Man (FRNM) with Rhine as its chief executive. A few minute's walk away is the Psychical Research Foundation established under an endowment from Charles Ozanne and headed by W. G. Roll, a former colleague of Rhine's. There could be no greater contrast between Rhine and Roll, FRNM and PRF. Rhine is elderly, fatherly, awesome, almost fearsome. Speaking with him is like talking to a living legend. Roll on the other hand is middle-aged, chummy, brotherly, and perky. FRNM's research is directed to the rigid, almost behavioristic experimental study of ESP and PK (psychokinesis) in the laboratory. PRF's research is carried out on only one major aspect of parapsychology—research into psychic phenomena indicating that man survives death. This is a subject anathema to Rhine. Even the buildings in which these two organizations are housed reveal the striking contrast between them. FRNM is housed in a huge Southern mansion as imposing as Rhine himself. PRF consists of two frame houses leased from Duke University which even now are scheduled to be torn down. In essence FRNM, like Rhine, is rigid and experimental. Mimicking Roll, PRF is idealistic, philosophical, and humanistic.

In my own mind my journey to Durham was not solely for research. I went with the same reverence and sense of duty as a Moslem making a pilgrimage to Mecca.

But this particular trip was to work with Blue Harary and his ability to induce the out-of-the-body experience. The OOBE is an experience in which an individual feels that his consciousness has become physically detached from the corporeal body. During this experience the subject reports the ability to move about freely in his fully awake consciousness, float about, move through walls and other physical obstructions, and travel great distances. According to surveys taken on the subject, the experience is very common and the experiencer finds himself enclosed either in an apparitional body, a ball or shaft of light, or sometimes merely as pure consciousness. Reporters also describe entering into telepathic, altered, and even mystical states of consciousness during the experience. OOBEs are prolifically recorded by people who have gone through a pseudodeath, almost drowned, during severe illness, or upon entering sleep.

The first thing the skeptic will charge is that the experiencer is really undergoing a mental aberration or "disturbance of body image," a psychotic delusion in which perception of the body is wildly distorted and which may lead to the delusion of being without a body. However, this charge does not explain the facts. The OOBE seems a common phenomenon. In 1936 A. Angyal published a paper in the *Archives of Neurology of Psychiatry* showing that distortion of body image was not common among psychotics. A 1964 report by S. Fischer in the *Archives of General Psychiatry* confirmed Angyal's statements. Distortion of body image is more frequent in chronically depressed people and in normal people under severe stress. But the incidence of the OOBE in the normal population seems irrefutably more widespread and of a phenomenologically different nature than body image distortion.

However, more important than trying to differentiate between OOBEs and body image disturbances is the wide variety of evidence that the OOBE is a psychic state; that is, it is inherently related to ESP and PK. People undergoing the OOBE report that they can travel great distances and observe incidents occurring there. Laboratory tests have also been run in which OOBEers have correctly perceived objects or a list of numbers in other rooms placed on high shelves out of eye range. In older writings on the OOBE it was claimed that during this state one could influence material objects that would be observed as telekinesis by an on-looker. Finally many people reporting OOBE have been seen as apparitions of the living, and some of the early French psychical researchers claimed that they had photographed the "astral body."

This rich parapsychological literature on the OOBE was ne-glected for decades until only recently when researchers began to explore this experience again. This new research has been focused on psychics who claim the ability to induce the OOBE *at will;* that is, they can induce it voluntarily, unlike most people who have no control over the experience at all. It occurs spontaneously, is brief, and rarely occurs again. However, a few gifted subjects not only can induce it at will, but also can prolong the experience, experi-ment, carry out prearranged tasks while in the state, and carry back a perfect recollection of the experience upon returning to the body.

During the summer of 1973 I worked with Blue consistently, lit-erally living with him for several weeks, experimented with him, socialized with him, philosophized with him, and explored every aspect of his OOB talents that I could. The OOBE has always fas-cinated me and is rather a specialty of mine. Several years ago I had a rash of OOBEs myself which increased my interest in this phase of parapsychology. When I went to Durham I went not only as a scholar on the history and literature on the OOBE, but also as one with some personal experience with the phenomenon. Despite these two assets, working with Blue proved to be an eye-opener.

The research with Blue is actually a threefold story: the chroni-cle of our experiments with him, Blue's own personal experiences and philosophy, and the curious way in which the money for this research was found. It is this last aspect of the Harary story that should first be given briefly.

The story begins with an eccentric Arizona prospector named James Kidd. Almost a recluse, Kidd disappeared in 1949 and was later declared legally dead. At this time it was discovered that he actually had a storehouse of wealth in spite of living in near squa-lor; the total estate was worth a quarter million dollars. Kidd had no heirs and his will was curious to say the least. It stated that his money should go to anyone who had done "research on some scientific proof of a soul in the human body which leaves at death." In 1967 hearings were begun which became known as "The Great Soul Trial."

When it became common knowledge that the money was up for grabs, several claimants applied. These included psychologists, philosophers, religious organizations, crackpots, and two parapsychological organizations, the American Society for Psychical Research and the Psychical Research Foundation.

At the hearing both the ASPR and the PRF offered expert witness to the fact that parapsychology had the history and resources necessary to tackle the problem. Clearly, any scientific research into survival of death would very well be within the range of the subjects studied in parapsychology. Even though most of parapsychology today is devoted to ESP and PK research, only psychical research was dedicated to the study of apparitions, hauntings, claims that the dead could communicate to the living through certain psychics, et al. There is no doubt that the study of survival after death is primarily the concern of parapsychology and that organized parapsychology was one of the few claimants with any legitimate claim to the money. But the way in which the parapsychological community went about trying to procure the money was almost comical, since survival research has been very much frowned upon for many decades. Chief witness for the ASPR was Dr. Gardner Murphy, who although himself very unsympathetic to the survival issue, eloquently argued that parapsychology had indeed a history of the study of mediumship, apparitions, deathbed visions, all of which was scientific research on the nature of death and survival. Murphy also spent much time discussing the OOBE, a topic toward which he has been unfavorable in his written essays, as a fruitful way of scientifically researching "the soul" and one of the best ways to tackle the problem.

The PRF's main spokesman was J. G. Pratt, and indeed PRF did lay better claim to the Kidd money than the ASPR. The PRF was endowed specifically to carry out survival research, and its project director, W. G. Roll had long been interested in that type of research. Of Danish birth, he had come to the United States from England (where he took an advanced degree in philosophy specializing in parapsychology) to work with J. B. Rhine. Since Rhine's research was oriented toward experimental ESP and PK, Roll soon left and under the Ozanne grant became the chief brains behind the PRF which soon grew into a major parapsychological organization. Pratt, although never in his long career had he ever fully engaged in survival research except for a few mediumistic experiments at the beginning, gave the same type of talk to the court as had Murphy.

At the end of the long hearings Judge Myers awarded the money to the Barrow Neurological Institute of Phoenix to carry out neurological research. In light of the testimony the choice was not only a poor one, but the Institute had damned itself by declaring that it had no strategy, nor concern, to carry out research into survival of death. The Arizona Supreme Court felt the same way and when the case was appealed, reversed the decision, stating, "At least two of the appellants, the American Society for Psychical Research, Inc., and the Psychical Research Foundation, Inc., are qualified to carry out the specific purpose expressed in the will."

In July 1971 Judge Myers reruled and granted the money to the ASPR which, in turn, requisitioned a large part of the Kidd estate to the PRF in order to carry out survival research jointly. And it was to the study of the OOBE that both organizations turned.

Blue Harary enters the picture as a result of this dual OOB project. Blue volunteered his services to the ASPR as an OOBE subject just at the time they were looking for OOBEers, and was tested by the ASPR team consisting mainly of Dr. Karlis Osis, director of research, and his assistant, Janet Mitchell, a hardworking graduate psychology student. These tests with Blue have not been published, but they consisted of his entering into the OOB state and trying to float above his body to report on target objects placed on a shelf suspended from the ceiling or report on pictures seen through a hole in a box while out of body. The shelf was in such a position as to be accessible only by ESP or through viewing it in the OOB state. During the entire test period Blue was monitored by psychophysiological devices such as the electroencephalograph, a brain-wave recording apparatus, and the polygraph. By the use of the EEG, et al., a psychologist or technician can determine what state of consciousness (waking, sleep, dreaming, and so forth) the subject is in, since each of these states have indicative rhythms. When I flew to Durham I stopped over in New York and talked with Dr. Osis and Miss Mitchell specifically about Blue. Janet told me that Blue had been sporadically successful on the target studies and had been able to report, although distortedly, on the shelf targets. Osis showed less enthusiasm about the target studies, even though the first test had been strikingly successful, but admitted that the psychophysiological readings offered curious results.

Because of his college work, Blue decided his best bet would be to go to Durham and enroll at Duke University so he could both further his education and take part in parapsychological research. He first approached the FRNM, but his talents were not particularly suited for the types of ESP projects carried out there, so ultimately he became established at PRF. His entry through PRF's door was the beginning of the most amazing and fruitful OOB experiments ever undertaken.

The task of organizing and designing the experiments fell to PRF's research coordinator, Dr. Robert Morris, a veteran parapsychologist and animal behaviorist. (His Ph.D. dissertation in biological psychology was on the mating habits of ringed-necked doves.) The first experiments were designed to substantiate that Blue could induce some sort of mind-beyond-the-body state. To reach this goal, the first series of tests were on target studies. In OOB research, this simply means the ability of the subject to travel in the OOB state and report on what he sees in an isolated, sealed-off room. Since the PRF consisted of two adjacent buildings, Blue merely induced the OOB state in one building and then traveled over to the next building and tried to see the target. Later, Blue OOBed from various Duke University buildings about half a mile away. In these experiments the targets were large posters of colored alphabet letters hung on a wall or door of the experimental area.

The first trial was on February 13, 1973, at 7:30 p.m. Blue lay down in one PRF building, hooked up to several psychophysiological recording devices and while still conscious began to sink into the ultrarelaxed state during which he leaves his body. This entire "cool down" period, as it was dubbed, lasts anywhere up to fifteen minutes. Blue reported that while out of the body he saw a circle as the target, slightly elliptical in shape, and a flowerpot. When Blue returned to his body and merged back to full consciousness, he was shown a series of potential target drawings from which he had to choose what he thought to be the correct one. Among these targets were drawings of a flowerpot and a circle. Blue chose the flowerpot. This was a disappointment since the target had been a circle. This first experiment provoked the touchy question that Blue might be using ESP during his OOBEs which would be a complicating factor in trying to demonstrate experimentally the validity of the OOBE on the basis of target studies. Another complication to the experiment was that one of the experimenters, Joseph Janis, a PRF staff member in the target room, had a subjective impression when Blue was "present" in the room with him which was borne out when the timings of the OOBE were worked out.

During the second experiment Blue began to focus in on the target better and, as in the first experiment, Joseph Janis was babysitting the target room. As Blue records in his diary of these experiments, he was able to quickly induce the OOB state and travel to the target room.

"The room was very cold and uncomfortable. I felt pressure but put it and everything else that was on my mind aside. Finally got to Joe and stayed there. Only saw the target briefly and then my "back" was to it. What I saw looked like a "V." Color was hard to see since perhaps the lighting was poor. Stood in front of Joe and looked at his face. Tried to signal him and got excited over finding that I actually could touch him! So I flew right back to the ol' body."

Blue signaled Dr. Morris and wrote down his impressions. The target was a "W." Blue was getting closer.

After a saddening failure on the third try, the fourth experiment perked up again.

"Left body and went to Joe (did not pass "go"—did not collect two hundred bucks). Actually, I had gone to Joe for a brief second . . . I was behind Joe's left side in the air. He seemed to get up out of his body when I came in, turned and found me and then continued turning and reentered his body. I didn't see anything on the door at all at first. Concentrated harder and thought I saw a vague image of a circle—an even vaguer Z. It was very difficult to see anything and I wondered if I was actually seeing what I thought I had been seeing (for a moment). Saw a person to Joe's right side and focused back in on Joe to maintain the experience.* Got tired and came back into body. . . ."

After returning to the body Blue induced a second OOBE, focused on Joseph Janis, and saw a vague "K." The actual target was an "R," so Blue's perception seemed to be a distorted version of the target set for him. However, what was even more fascinating was that on his first visit he had reported a second person in the target area with Joe. After the experiment had ended, it was revealed that a second person *had* been introduced into the target area unbeknownst to Blue, a PRF volunteer, Jerry Posner. What's more, during the test Jerry Posner reported to Joe that he "saw" Blue's apparition. Joe Janis made a recording of the time and this directly correlated to when Blue was actually OOBing, a time unknown to either Joe or Jerry. When I questioned Jerry about the experiment, he described how he was startled to see a clear apparitional representation of Blue's face hovering in the air. Indeed, at this point, the Harary experiments were entering into a new phase.

The March 18 experiment was a clear success and Blue was able to report the target precisely:

"The experiment was from one PRF building to the other. I had

* Blue likes to focus in on a person to whom he feels close during the test. It helps him reach the target area and maintain the OOB state while there.

some difficulty relaxing at first but put personal problems out of my mind and focused in on being a whole human being and was able to relax. I signaled Bob [Morris] when ready and went to the center of the room (OOBE) to look at the target. It was a little dim at first but I got used to the light and saw it after a while. It was a blue arrow pointing up."

The entire series gave a good number of approximate and precise "hits" but did not seem totally suited to Blue's OOB abilities, since he often had trouble "seeing" and often perceived objects distortedly. However, he had been a bit more successful at identifying the correct color of the letters than the letters themselves.

The experiences of Joe Janis and Jerry Posner alerted Dr. Morris and other PRF researchers to the fact that Blue might be more able to make his presence known to people or animals than reporting on targets. Further, if Blue could be detected habitually by humans, this would be stronger evidence than target studies that he was somehow physically or ultraphysically present in the target area. Merely describing target objects could be ESP. So, for the next phase, "detectors" were used, usually PRF staff members or volunteers. For these experiments Blue would travel to one of the PRF buildings where he was to report on whom he saw in the experimental area and their relative positions. At the same time it was hoped that the detectors could "sense" when Blue was present. Usually three people would be randomly selected and positioned in the area. At first Blue was successful at reporting their positions, but even though this ability soon tapered off, some of the detectors did have visual or subjective sensations of his presence during the time Blue visited the target area while in an OOB state. The detectors only knew that, in a given period of time (thirty to forty minutes, for example), Blue would OOB over for a minute or so. They were, of course, kept in the dark as to the precise time. Again, at first, some detectors were highly successful, sensing Blue, seeing sparkling lights, or even an apparition. Jerry Posner was the most successful. But as might be expected, the detectors began to get self-conscious about their task and wound up "guessing" when they thought Blue was present, eventually losing the ability to relax and remain preoccupied or unattentive to the experiment, all of which seem to facilitate any ESP function. However, although the detectors themselves often became too attentive, the people running the experiments, although not detectors, began having fairly strong detection experiences themselves. This type of peripheral detection became prevalent in all the Harary work. For example, when Dr. Morris began using animals as detectors, he went through a detection period himself. As Dr. Morris told me, "During one of these periods I experienced the feeling that Blue was in some sense there. It was not a strong impression, but it did impel me to make note of it at the time. My experience was totally internal—no sensations, visual or otherwise, involved. I thought of Blue, thought about the possibility that Blue might be having an OOBE at the time. I felt very comfortably warm inside, a good feeling, as I would if I knew I were being visited by a friend. The feeling lasted no more than twenty to thirty seconds. I realized that I knew the odds were 50-50 that Blue was in fact experiencing an OOBE at the time and that my description's main value was therefore the comparability of its details with other descriptions obtained under more impressive circumstances."

The use of human detectors had stagnated, so the next phase of the research was to use animals, and at first gerbils and hamsters were enlisted. For the experiments the rodent would be placed inside a 6″ × 6″ × 6″ wire cage on top of a "jiggle platform." This consisted of a triangularly shaped metal base delicately balanced on ball bearings. When an animal moved about in this cage, the amount of motion could be recorded on a polygraph to which it can be hooked. In this way, one could judge those times when the animal speeded up or slowed down its movements significantly. Morris had previously found that small animals were able to show ESP by significantly slowing or speeding up their activity rates during more conventional animal-ESP (an-psi) research. It was hoped that when Blue projected, the little rodents would interrupt their normal behavior. For the experiment a forty-minute detection period was agreed upon. About four feet away from the detection area an assistant would continuously record the animals' overt behavior. Blue was situated at Duke University, half a mile away, and at a randomly determined time would try to influence the animals' behavior while in the OOB state. Unfortunately, the gerbils did not respond at all, although Blue told me that once one of the rodents did perk up and stare directly at him during the test.

The failure of the gerbils and hamsters to respond might have been foreseen, though, for the creatures are very gentle and tame animals that habituate easily to human beings around them. Perhaps they merely found nothing unusual about Blue's sudden OOB appearances. Perhaps, too, it would have been better to use animals more readily influenced by Blue—a pet that would react more openly. And it was the use of Blue's own pets that offered the most striking experimental results.

To facilitate these tests, Blue adopted two kittens. When he first approached the litter, one kitten unhesitatingly and inquisitively ventured forward. Another soon followed the first, and these two were chosen since Blue felt the first kitten's strong initial response to him would carry over more favorably into the formal experiments. The second kitten was kept on as a playmate for the first. The kittens were appropriately named, Spirit and Soul. It was Spirit, the first inquisitive fur-ball that became PRF's star OOB detector.

For the experiments Dr. Morris used an animal activity board, an oblong shuffle-board-like apparatus (30″ × 80″) marked off into twenty-four numbered, ten-inch squares. As with the gerbil experiments, the cats could be observed as they ran about the board. A reporter could keep track over how many squares the kittens ventured during a given period and the amount of "meows" evoked. This would give a base-line figure of the kitten's normal activity rate. The tests were comprised of four experimental periods, and during two of them (determined randomly) Blue would try to project from Duke Hospital to PRF and visit the kittens. The results were amazing. During the first test, Spirit, usually an energy-charged, all-American kitten, suddenly calmed down, immediately stopped meowing, and ceased dashing over the activity board. It was determined that at this very time Blue had projected to it.

Because of the strong response to Blue, a series was run just with Spirit. As usual, four time periods were used, with only two comprising the OOB attempts and the observers were kept ignorant of these times. During the experimental periods Spirit would dart about, try to escape from the apparatus, and vocalize regularly. However, in Blue's OOB presence, the cat would cease all activity, calmly sit, and remain perfectly quiet. For example, during the total control periods, Spirit meowed thirty-seven times; during the OOB periods, exactly none. Figured statistically the results were astoundingly above what one would have expected by chance.

During these experiments some of the observers also detected Blue. It was Jerry Levin's duty to monitor some of the physical devices (thermistors and the like) to see if Blue would influence them during the animal experiments. Jerry was a talented young PRF worker and an undergraduate student in psychology who took part in several of the OOB experiments. On one occasion he had a vivid detection of Blue during one of the animal studies. His report reads:

> On the night of July 5 our experiment involved human, animal and physical detectors. A kitten was placed in an "open field" situation, its behavior observed by D.E. [Debbi Ewers] and R.M. [Robert Morris]. On a table next to the open field apparatus was placed a thermistor, insulated from air currents by Styrofoam and being monitored in the next room on a polygraph. I was operating the polygraph, seated in front of it, with no one else present in the room. All the people involved were instructed to note the time and character of any possible detection of the OOBer that they might have.
>
> The experimental design was such that there were four, two minute detection periods. . . . He [Blue] would actually have an OOBE two out of the four detection periods. None of the detectors knew which period, as they were determined by a flip of a coin in the other building. In addition to the detection periods a warning period of varying length

was used to obtain control data just before the detection period. I was just at the end of the first warning period when I saw a black streak in the periphery of my vision. Phenomenologically, the sensation appeared to be a thin black line about a foot away, between me and the polygraph. It was as if it were a fast moving black point leaving an after image behind. The streak was about the length of a pencil and lasted no more than a second. It was a very well-defined sensation which faded quickly. My impression was that the streak was an after image of some metallic part of the polygraph—there was a dim light in the room. I noted briefly the time and character of the sensation and went back to monitoring the polygraph. After the experiment was over we learned that the OOBE had just started at the time of my detection response. That was my only detection response during that session.

Blue's OOBE had been unusually vivid that night and he described how he easily induced an OOBE lasting about five minutes. His vision was clear and he experienced himself as "a large, glowing ball of greenish tinted light which appeared to be about the size of a standard beach ball." He traveled to the experimental area, saw Spirit sitting calmly, and then returned to his body. Later he learned of the strong response by the kitten, corresponding to what he had observed, and of Jerry Levin's visual detection.

It was with all this material in mind that I went to Durham. I had heard quite a bit about Blue from Bob Morris over the phone and from Janet Mitchell at the ASPR. I landed in Durham and was met by Bob and Blue. One usually expects a certain aura of theatrics when meeting a gifted psychic. Many of them talk incessantly, always about themselves, boast, and offer long recitations and credits. But there was none of this in Blue. He was quiet, almost reticent about his experiences; thoughtful; and very concerned with making me at home. He was living at the PRF's building and I was billeted in the meditation center behind the PRF's offices and separated from them by a grass quad. During the next six weeks Blue was my constant companion. We spent much of our time together, ate together, rambled about Durham together, and most important, experimented together. But it was not a case of a researcher and a subject. It was instead a collaboration based on mutual trust and friendship, each of us taking joy in the adventure of discovery.

My own introduction to the experiments was that same night. It was not part of a formal series, but was to see if Jerry Posner's dog would react to Blue's presence. The dog slept blissfully throughout the entire period which nullified any hopes of getting a strong reaction, but half a mile away I was able to watch Blue in action. He entered an isolation booth at the psychophysiological laboratory in the engineering building at Duke. He doesn't like to be watched during the OOB trial, so his voice is monitored through an intercom. As Blue relaxes he often gives little sighs and finally he whispers over the intercom a word such as "soon"—and then silence. Blue is "out." Several minutes later he'll whisper again, tell his account, and then emerge from the lab. Usually he is dissociated, walks unevenly, his vision is distorted. It takes him a few minutes to get back to normal and he sometimes feels pain in his chest, ranging from slight aches to recurrent jabbing pain.

My own work with Blue was carried out in conjunction with Bob Morris and again an animal was used. I had discussed various ideas with Bob about animal experimentation. My own view was this: perhaps the use of kittens or any domesticated animal was really moving in the wrong direction. These animals are used to humans and might not react to an OOB presence. Instead I felt that an animal that was distrustful or vigilant in the presence of people might be the best bet. Such an animal might react more violently to an intruder than a pet or an experimental animal such as a gerbil or hamster. My theory was in keeping with Bob's plans since a member of Durham's parapsychological elite, Graham Watkins, was an animal behaviorist with a penchant for snakes. Graham had one exceptional snake that seemed right up our alley and had already offered to lend it to us. Graham had found the snake lying by the roadside and had merely picked it up to add to his collection. But the reptile's initial calm demeanor was atypical. No sooner had it been placed in captivity than it showed the orneriest, most vigilant disposition imaginable. It never habituated to humans at all and would become alert at the slightest provocation. If held with a rubber glove, it would constantly attack and bite the gloved hand while most snakes give up when they find their attack fruitless. The snake would strike at the glass terrarium in which it was housed if a hand came too close to it. The snake was ideal for our purposes.

For the first experiment Blue, Bob, and Graham went over to the Duke Hospital. I remained at PRF as chief observer with Jerry Posner and, of course, the snake. The PRF building has a small isolation booth in which the snake was placed in its wood-shaving-filled terrarium. The booth has a large window through which I could watch the snake. Bright lights were focused on the snake from my position in the room so it could not possibly be alerted or influenced by my actions. As usual, there were four experimental periods. A phone signal cued us when a period was to begin, and Jerry signaled to me the completion of every ten-second time period of the three-minute session. Of course neither of us knew in which of the periods Blue would make his attempts.

During the entire duration of the experiment, the snake made only one odd response which was noted by me at that time. Before the experiment I had observed the snake as it calmly explored its cage. During the first three-minute experimental period, the snake made no overt or unusual response. Although unknown to me at the time, no OOBE had taken place during the first period. However, shortly after the beginning of the second experimental period, the snake began to speed up its activity rate and, stretching out completely, burrowed under the shavings at the bottom of the cage. The snake had done this during the preexperimental observation period while it explored its new home, but not with such violence or speed. After quickly burrowing, the snake started upward at the top of the cage, resting its head, throat forward, on the glass side. There it remained motionless for a moment, then quickly slid up the side of the cage (the side closest to me) until it was halfway up the glass. It then gnawed and bit wildly at the glass as though attacking something, or trying to "eat through" the glass. This lasted for about twenty to thirty seconds. The snake then suddenly became calm again. This reaction occurred right in the middle of a three-minute experimental session. Prior to the experiment the snake had on two occasions opened its mouth and placed it against the glass. However, in both cases these reactions lasted only for a few seconds at most with no concomitant speedup of activity rate. After the violent reaction, the snake only opened its mouth on one other occasion.

When Blue, Bob, and Graham returned to the PRF we correlated times. It was a grand-slam home run. During the second period Blue had projected and reported that he had visited the snake immediately after the beginning of the period. Before visiting the reptile he had floated about the room occupied by Jerry and me, hoping to get our attention. After using up several seconds in this attempt, he focused attention on the snake but did not record any specific action by it. By comparing Bob's timing to my own we found an almost exact correspondence. (During the fourth experimental period Blue reported a brief OOBE to our area.) We were all very excited about the success (or at least most of us were; no one bothered to ask the snake) and were eager to replicate the test.

Graham also had carried out an impromptu test that had shown some unusual results. He had left two electrodes from the polygraph open to pick up white noise in the room. During the two OOB periods the noise level in the room housing Blue recorded a significant alteration. This would indicate that Blue's OOB manifestation caused an alteration in the atmosphere of the room (such as a change in the ozone level). That is, if no other cause could be found. When Graham mentioned ozone to me I became excited, for during experiments carried out in France during the 1920s and 1930s with physical mediums, it was often reported that the odor of ozone pervaded the room, heralding any phenomena. Could there be an important parallel here? Unfortunately, Graham's recordings were too vague to provide even a cursory attempt at isolating the variable that Blue was affecting, and this was never followed up. But it remains a tantalizing pointer to something about the energy source of Blue's OOBE. Could he be taking power from the atmosphere in order to manifest outside his body? If Blue needed an energy source to manifest his consciousness apart from the body, there would be the requisite free-floating energy in the atmosphere. If Blue does utilize this energy about him when he travels out of the body, one should expect a slight change in temperature in his general area since as energy is extracted from the air it automatically cools. Another OOB traveler, Ingo Swann, Karlis Osis' prize subject, had already carried out PK tasks trying to raise the temperature of pieces of Bakelite and graphite. When he succeeded, thermistors hooked to outlying and nontarget pieces of material dropped in temperature. This indicated that somehow, through PK, Swann had used energy in the air, transformed it and redirected it by PK which while raising the temperature in the target area, decreased the temperature in the outlying area. Does Blue use the same type of energy to manifest beyond his body? There is some tantalizing evidence that he does. Jerry Levin hooked up delicate thermistors in the experimental area during the animal tests. On one occasion (and one occasion only, alas) the thermistor did record dips in temperature when Blue approached it. One might also add that during hauntings these temperature drops have been recorded. And with the famous medium, Stella C., Harry Price, the British psychical investigator, photographed thermometers systematically dropping in temperature during her séances and as telekinetic movements erupted in the séance room. Blue's freak actuation of the thermistor is consistent with a whole range of findings in parapsychology and leads me to think that he manifests himself by the use of physical energy, using it to become semiphysical during this OOB state. (As most experiencers, Blue sees himself as traveling in the OOB state alternately as an apparitional body, as an orb or shaft of light, or just as pure consciousness.)

A few days later we replicated the snake experiment, using the same procedure as before. But during the preexperimental period the snake burrowed into the shavings and never stirred for the rest of the test. It apparently slept, ruining the entire experiment.

Unfortunately, summer is always a hectic time in parapsychology, for the end of summer brings with it the annual convention of the Parapsychological Association. As the convention serves as the meeting ground for the exchange of ideas and the presentation of new research, summer is often a mad rush to finish up research, get it analyzed and written up in time for the convention. The PRF was in the same bind since two research briefs were to be given on Blue. This forestalled concentration on long experimental series, so we never ran a replication of the snake test. Further experiments with Blue had to be almost informal and the following researches were nearly one-shot deals.

I must admit that I have a fondness for target studies. To be sure, animal detection experiments are much more suggestive that the subject is really leaving the body and traveling than are target studies. But somehow there seems to be an element of uncertainty with animal studies. Animals are unpredictable. Can we really judge their behavior objectively? Are we really only inferring that they are being affected by the OOBEer? If I were to design an experimental project with Blue, I would use animal detectors as Bob Morris did. There is no doubt that, evaluated scientifically, this design gets to the meat of the OOBE better than target studies. But, if Blue were to go to a target area and describe accurately what was there, there could be no room for error in ascertaining that he had accomplished something extraordinary. To the experimenter the evidence from a well-designed target study can be more stunning and concrete than watching meditative cats or uptight snakes.

Blue has no special love for target studies. He feels they put him on a spot and places him in a position where he has to "prove" himself. Nonetheless, during my Durham stay I did constantly urge Blue to do some target studies with me. Since the formal detection experiments were in abeyance while all the technical details on their findings were being written up, Blue acquiesced to my request and we were able to carry out two target studies with the assistance of Bob.

For the first test on August 14 I remained at PRF while Bob and Blue were at Duke Hospital. The experiment was twofold; first, to permit me to carry out a target test while allowing Blue to become accustomed to a new apparatus Graham had developed. This odd-looking contraption consisted of a rotund cage with a bottom of depressible, pie-shaped planks. When an animal runs about the cage, it depresses the planks and an exact record of the animal's movements is punched out. We hoped to use this with the animal experiments. The top was screened over. After Blue left I randomly picked out several objects to decorate the top of the unit with. I could have used anything in the PRF buildings. At the left rear of the unit I placed a large bottle sandwiched between two Frisbees lying flat down. As a musician, I had brought an instrument with me, an oboe. Blue had been interested in the long black wooden instrument, and I felt he might easily focus in on it. The oboe was assembled, placed on its open black rectangular case and put *inside* the apparatus, but not obstructed by the bottle and Frisbees. And then I waited.

Bob called me from Duke Hospital at 9:46 P.M. to synchronize our clocks. At 10:11 Blue induced a three-minute OOBE and at 10:14 reported the following impressions which were written down at the time by Bob. Italicized portions represent correct responses by Blue or descriptions remarkably similar to the objects I had chosen for the test:

"Got down deep, flip over there, real deep when there, T.V. looked on. Looked around room, above and around apparatus. Hard to see. *Round flat object like plate to front right in apparatus.** Maybe glass.* Hard to remember. *Something black and square diagonally.* Unclear. *Saw two things: both might have been same thing. Something tall standing in middle.* Might have created a kitten. *Long pencil on top. Something round.* Not the piece of wood, *maybe a frisbee on top.*"

* Blue often has a reversal of sight or mirror vision during his OOBEs which would account for his correct description but incorrect placement of the object.

After a few comments about his internal experiences Blue reported: *"Maybe saw bottle.* Shoe on top, to the right."

As the reader can see, Blue's impressions and language are confused. This is to be expected since he is in a very dazed condition when he returns to the body and has to report on his experiences. But, sorting through the impressions it is remarkable how most of them are on dead center. Blue's reporting of a "round flat object like plate" and then "saw two things; both might have been same thing" are obvious and direct references to the two Frisbees. Eventually Blue was able to name the objects correctly. He initially reported seeing "maybe glass" and again described seeing the bottle. For one not familiar with musical instruments, his attempt at describing my oboe was successful. The case is jet black and rectangular. "Something tall in the middle" could easily relate to the long thin shape of the oboe which Blue probably perceived in the wrong perspective. This comment is augmented by his description of a "long pencil on top." It appears that Blue was "seeing" the target objects, but did not perceive them as we do with our normal vision. Instead he seems to be seeing one-dimensionally as though he did not have stereoscopic vision as we all do in our physical bodies.

When Blue returned with Bob to the PRF, I had set up a collection of objects from which Blue was to choose the target objects. Although his layout was different than mine, he chose six out of nine objects as the likely targets of which five were the ones I had actually used. (Blue chose an additional object, a pair of black gloves which he placed with the oboe case because of their color.) He correctly ascertained that the oboe was *within* the cage not atop it accompanying the other objects, although he thought it was standing upright not laid flat. (And the TV had not been turned on.) *

The test also gave me a chance to find out if suggestion played a part in Blue's OOBEs. Could he be suggestioned into seeing certain objects during his often opaque OOB vision? When Blue, Bob,

---

* It should be noted that when Blue made his decision about which objects I had used for the test, I had *already left* the room. In this respect he could not have chosen the objects by watching me for unconscious visual cues.

and I had designed the test and when Bob suggested that I choose PRF objects, I intentionally glanced over to a large globe in Bob's office. I made sure that Blue caught my eye and saw me glance at the globe. I wanted to see if somehow this "cue" would influence him to report seeing a globe. Such an impression might easily lodge and distort the impressions of someone using ESP. As can be seen, Blue rejected this cue totally which impressed me very much.

The next target study was carried out using the same design. Unfortunately there was a storm brewing and Blue is reluctant about OOBing during electrical storms. Although he did project to the apparatus again, he reported to Bob only a very vague vision and specifically stated that he felt he had not been able to perceive the targets and the test was a failure from an evidential standpoint, although it is highly significant that Blue successfully predicted that he had done poorly. My target studies followed the same hex that plagued all my work with Blue—a fascinating initial test but circumstances circumventing the opportunity for a follow-up. Since Blue had no love for target studies, we discontinued the tests even though he had certainly astounded me with his first target descriptions.

Up to this point my experiences with Blue had verified two facets of his abilities—effecting animal detectors and seeing at a distance. There was one other prime facet of his abilities that was fascinating—the visual detection of his OOB form by human witnesses. Although Blue often tried to make his presence known, it was only on occasion that people actually were able to detect his form, and these were usually only peripherally as in Jerry Levin's case. Friends of Blue, Jerry Posner for one, recorded more vivid experiences. Blue records often traveling as a shaft or ball of light and reports that he can take apparitional form at will. Several close friends of his have reported, anecdotally, visual sightings in keeping with Blue's self-perception.

On my first day in Durham, Blue introduced me to Debbi Ewers, whom he saw quite often, and she recounted to me a particularly vivid experience which she associated with Blue.

It was 4:30 in the morning and I was literally exhausted. But the feeling of exhaustion was a rather pleasant one because I had just spent 10 very happy and peaceful hours with Blue. I had been in bed for only 10 minutes—when I saw a light up in the corner of the room near the ceiling. It was *not* a light that was flat on the wall, but one that was soft white and spherical that was dim and then grew brighter. It grew dim again and then very bright when I mentally "spoke" to it. I assumed it was Blue. The light never changed its position in the room, only its intensity. When I began to get frightened (because this kind of thing hadn't happened before), I mentally "said" so, and it gradually faded away and I felt very peaceful again. This experience lasted at least twenty seconds. The light, at its peak intensity, appeared maybe two feet in diameter.

Miss Ewers was one of PRF's most successful detectors although she functioned not only as a detector but as an experimenter. Her job was to announce to the formal human detectors the beginning and end of a forty-minute experimental period during which Blue was to OOB-in twice at randomly chosen times. While engaging in unrelated activities while running the test, she twice felt the presence of someone invisible in the room. "It was an indescribable feeling of the room being 'full' as opposed to 'empty,' " and she even saw a blue circular light hovering for a second. Miss Ewers made a note of the times and both correlated precisely with Blue's OOB visits.

It was the day before I left Durham for Los Angeles that I ultimately was able to have one of these visual detections myself. Blue's farewell gift to me couldn't have been more apropos or welcomed. I had been with him that evening and at 11:30 P.M. decided to retire for the night at the meditation center. Blue usually stays up till 4:00 or 5:00 in the morning and then sleeps well into the afternoon. I went to bed but sleep wasn't easy that night and I found myself still half-awake, tossing and turning at 3:15 A.M. (I have a habit of checking my wristwatch, which I wear even when sleeping, as soon as I wake at any time. So this timing is very precise.) I couldn't get comfortable and tossed, turned, and rolled all over the bed, still drowsy, but awake. I was shifting from my right side to my left when out of the corner of my eye I saw a hovering red light. It was not reflected on the wall and my brief glimpse indicated it to be between my bed and the door of the bedroom diagonally across the room which leads to a hallway. The ball was red and may even have been two orbs joined together. It was uncanny and it darted or streaked across the room and disappeared in the same manner as had Jerry Levin's "shadow." I was still groggy but literally catapulted out of bed and rushed to my desk to make a note of the time. It was almost an autonomic reaction. I didn't decide to get out of bed, I just found myself rushing to the desk almost as if I had started from the bed before becoming sufficiently awake. It can best be compared to suddenly finding yourself out of bed running to answer a ringing telephone in the middle of the night with no real recollection of getting out of bed. I merely wrote down, "thought I saw a red light in my peripheral vision" and noted the time. It was 3:22 A.M. Then I went back to bed.

The next morning I had a meeting to attend, and when I returned to the PRF buildings that afternoon, Blue was standing on the porch watching me with his usual implike grin protruding through his close-cropped beard. He had just gotten up and didn't say anything to me at all. I was hoping, praying, that he would report his OOBE to me, but he didn't. Finally I asked him if he had had an OOBE after he had gone to bed as he often does. Blue, still dazed from sleep, said he had, so again I waited in anticipation, hoping he would say something that would independently validate what I saw. But he didn't and so I finally had to ask him point-blank if he recalled projecting to my room. Blue thought for a minute, as though trying to latch onto a fleeting memory. Yes, he said, he did remember going to sleep telling himself he would try to visit me, vaguely remembered journeying to the meditation center, and then "flew off" to Virginia to see where he would be lodged during the Parapsychological Association convention to be held shortly in Charlottesville. He couldn't remember anything more. Because I had been forced to hint to Blue that I had had a detection, the evidence for the correspondence between my experience and Blue's was weakened. However, when I told him of the experience, but not the time, I asked him to try to determine the approximate time of his OOB visit. He thought for a few moments and then said that since the OOBE had taken place shortly after he had retired, and since he thought he had first visited me, he was able to isolate the time between 3:00 and 3:30 A.M. The timing was the key evidential factor since it corresponded roughly to my 3:22 A.M. sighting. In addition it is a bit unusual for Blue to retire so early (for him!).

Although my experience was ephemeral at best, it tallied with many other detections by PRF workers. Like Jerry Levin, I perceived Blue only out of the corner of my eye as something unusual streaked past. Like Jerry, the experience carried with it an inner compulsion to make a specific and exact note of the time. And like Jerry, Debbi, and many others, it took place while my mind was completely off making any attempt to detect him.

In each of the out-of-the-body trials Blue's psychophysiology was carefully recorded, both during the cool down periods and during the OOBEs. To get a firm idea of his bodily state during the experience, electroencephalograms were taken of the left and right hemispheres of his brain, skin potential, respiration, blood pulse volume, heart rate, eye movements, and muscle movements (EOG) were all monitored.

These readings are vastly complex, since to find correlations each recording must be compared to each of the same readings for every OOBE. Then various recordings must be correlated with other types of psychophysiological records to see if there are significant patterns between them and which might be direct links. Briefly, though, respiration, heart rate, and blood pulse increased significantly during the OOBE while the EOG and skin potential decreased.

Dr. Charles Tart of the University of California, Davis, has reported that with his two subjects the EEGs showed odd patterns when they induced the OOBE from the sleep state. A comparison of Blue's EEG between the cool down and OOB phases indicated little initial differences. However, when a more sensitive and exacting measurement was employed, the electrical activity of the left hemisphere of the brain showed a gradual decrease. This is in keeping with EEG monitoring and findings with Ingo Swann who also induces the experience from the waking state, although his shifts are more marked than Blue's.

Significantly, the patterns of Blue's OOBE psychophysiology were notably different from normal sleep and dreaming. His EEG tracings were those of a normal waking but relaxed state. Eye movements decreased during the OOBE while a proliferation of rapid eye movements is a prime dream trait. Blue's muscle tonus was notably relaxed, differing from both sleep and the effects of deep anesthesia. So we can be sure that, if anything, Blue is certainly not merely sleeping and dreaming with ESP during his out-of-the-body excursions.

All of these results will have to be more tightly analyzed before any meaningful correlates with the OOBE can be isolated. However, it might be significant to note that the increase in respiration and heartbeat and the decrease in mental activity are similar to Eastern breathing exercises which, if mastered, allegedly can induce the OOBE. It should also be mentioned that during the research analysis Blue was kept completely unaware about his own responses so that he would not, unconsciously or automatically, use some form of biofeedback to regulate his psychophysiology to conform to his own precedents.

Although I had to leave Durham and my work with Blue, I have not lost my fascination with the experimentation done there with him. With Bob Morris gradually withdrawing from the PRF to carry out independent research, Graham Watkins, John Hartwell, a psychophysiologist, and Joseph Janis, all of whom had previously worked with Blue, took over the experimentation. Graham's work was to use his animal monitoring unit described in my target studies to see if the animals would orient themselves in the direction of Blue. If he were to position his out-of-the-body self northward, would the cat do likewise? The first results looked promising, but then the star cat, Spirit, habituated to the apparatus quickly and would merely sit passively and not move at all immediately upon being placed in the cage. In order to readapt the experiments, a large room was used, monitored by closed-circuit TV, into which a cat was placed. Blue was to OOB over and stand randomly in one of the corners of the room. Again Blue's pets were used, and although no results were forthcoming—the cats roamed about totally impervious to Blue's presence—one of the technicians began to have strong detection experiences. At first he recorded his impressions as to which corner Blue was in, and in the four trials in which he ventured to place his impressions on record, he was 100 percent correct. During the last test the technician recorded seeing Blue's face over the monitor and again his report of the OOB presence was on target.

How can I sum up Blue parapsychologically and personally? Having had the experience myself during the years 1965–1967, I felt I had a good idea of what the OOBE was. To me, it seemed plain that when one is projecting out of the body, he is releasing some sort of ultraphysical "body" or apparition, semiphysical in nature. Blue's OOB talents radically altered my conception. My first change in position was to revise this rigid, confining view of the OOBE. To be sure, many persons undergoing this experience find themselves in a replica of the human body and, in fact, they are often seen as apparitions by observers. But Blue's experiences signaled to me a realization that the OOBE is not one experience, but a continuum of experiences. In this respect, as I mentioned earlier, Blue can travel as an "apparition," as a ball or shaft of light, or merely as a point of consciousness dangling in space. These are all OOBEs but of a different nature. There is no one prototype out-of-the-body experience; rather, there are varieties of out-of-body functioning.

Now, exactly what is the "space" to which we project during the OOBE? Here our own bias blinds us. Most people when undergoing the OOBE find themselves observing normal scenes—their own bedrooms, homes of friends, frequented haunts, and so forth. Logically, experiencers assume that they are projecting into the same physical space which our bodies occupy normally. But this may be a fallacy. Blue's experiences illustrated the paradox that while he was seeing our "real" world, the world he observed was slightly different. He might see furniture arranged incorrectly, nonexistent objects, or carry out actions that seem "physical" to him, but are not according to witnesses present. Blue told me that during one OOBE he snuffed out a candle. Yet upon reentering the body and awaking from a night's sleep, the candle had burned down to the candle base. Obviously his OOB act had carried no influence over the physical object whatsoever.

At first I was prone to think that these oddities were carry-overs from dream symbols, impressions or archetypes filtering in during the OOBE—in other words, the activity of the brain polluting the psychic perception of the OOBEer. But gradually I had to switch from this position entirely. Blue was not asleep during his OOBEs and still reported these odd inconsistencies. Finally, on some occasions during the animal detection experiments, although the animal *was* reacting to "something," Blue was reporting experiences in a totally unrecognizable world he had entered during his experience. He was with the animal, apparently ultraphysically, but even he could not recognize his position as such.

It is here that the writings of Professor J. H. M. Whiteman fall into the picture. Whiteman is a professor of mathematics and a scholar. He is also a habitual OOBEer and has described other-world encounters in his *The Mystical Life*. Whiteman argues that in order for us to judge the "realness" of an experience, we can only evaluate it in terms of how it relates to the "real" world. Because of this, when a person undergoes an OOBE, he perceives the world around him as though he were in physical space. However, what he is really contacting is a fourth-dimensional world which mimics the real world lying parallel to it and seeing etheric representations of physical objects and their environments, not the objects themselves. Whiteman also believes that, as one becomes more accustomed to accepting that he is really venturing into a new reality, he becomes less and less dependent on the "real" world and gradually experiences new levels of consciousness and many different "worlds" and environments contacted through the OOBE.

Whiteman's views are attractive and do explain Blue's own experiences and their often paradoxical and surrealistic quality. In order to test this theory about the OOBE that I had developed from Whiteman's writings and my observations with Blue, I began to restudy the experiences of a British occultist, Hugh Callaway, who wrote of his OOBEs under the pen name, Oliver Fox, in his *Astral Projection.** Fox recorded several OOBEs and dated them in his book. I arranged them chronologically and started mapping out their characteristics. As Fox began to have more and more OOBEs and as he became accustomed to the state, he began to have otherworld experiences that departed from merely experiencing the "real" world. Gradually he pulled further away from our physical world, having many more bizarre experiences, but with age these surrealistic qualities declined. When mapped on a graph, Fox's experiences reveal an asymmetrical incline and decline. To check to see whether his experiences were due to greater length and care taken in recording, I compared my first graph with a chart of the length of the narratives. No correlation was found between the amount of paradoxical experiences inconsistent with the real world (traveling through a hole in space, seeing nonexistent objects, and so forth) and length of description. A computer check of this data (correlation of coefficients) upheld this noncorrelation. It seems likely that, just as Whiteman claimed in his philosophy, the experiencer, in time, throws off the bias of the "real" world during the OOB state to explore unknown and challenging new dimensions. Perhaps the OOBE is just as personal an experience as the LSD experience, shaped and molded by the experiencer's own world view, psychological state, and expectations.

To view the OOBE in this light casts Blue Harary's experiences into a more understandable framework.

As I said, Blue is neither theatrical nor boastful of his abilities.

* Oliver Fox, *Astral Projection* (New York: University Books, 1962).

He is intrigued with them, yet he purposely shies away from reading the reports of others in order to keep from being influenced by them. He views himself as an experimenter, not as a subject, and takes an active role in designing and evaluating research carried out with him. In my own view, Blue is shy, retiring, sensitive, intelligent, and compassionate. His own writings are literary, his poetry delicate. Although a full-time college student in experimental psychology at Duke University, a research assistant at PRF and chief OOBEer-in-residence, he still takes the time to spend one entire night a week working at a crisis center answering calls from and counseling distressed people on the verge of everything from breakdown to suicide.

Blue's personal shyness is manifested several ways. He rarely talks about his experiences unless asked and will not discuss certain aspects of them which he feels are too personal. He is quite the antipathy of the usual psychic. He just looks you straight in the eye and in dead seriousness and with reverential awe narrates an encounter or view about his experiences or philosophies.

And that is the same manner I try to adopt when discussing the enigma of Blue Harary.

# 3

# In Search of Haunted Houses

What is a haunted house and how do you go about investigating one? A haunting can be defined simply as any abode in which outbreaks of psychic phenomena continually occur. These could include apparitions, noises, physical motion of objects, voices, breezes, and even odd subjective feelings. Usually in the course of a haunting, these effects will be witnessed by more than one occupant or visitor to the house.

What causes a haunting is just as mysterious as the phenomena it generates. At one time it was automatically assumed that hauntings were instigated by the spirits of the dead. However this explanation eventually gave way to the idea that if the house had been the site of tragic events it could be pervaded by some sort of psychic influence generated by the emotions accompanying these events. Sensitive people might come into contact with these impressions and experience the haunting. Finally it was suggested that hauntings were due to traces of past events registered directly onto the house which merely replay themselves sporadically.

Whatever the cause of hauntings they represent one of psychical research's most baffling mysteries as well as a terrifying ordeal for anyone who finds himself in the midst of one. It is here the psychical investigator most often gets involved, and this poses the second question: just how does one go about investigating a haunting?

There are three ways in which this problem has been handled in past investigations. The first technique is merely to investigate and interview all the witnesses, collect and evaluate their testimony, and, of course, check over the house to see if any normal cause could be responsible for the reported phenomena. This might include anything from perfectly natural but camouflaged physical causes to out-and-out fraud. And in my own experience the latter far outnumber the former. A second method of investigating a reportedly haunted house is based on the old tradition that animals react strangely to the supernormal. There seems good reason to believe that animals are hypersensitive to hauntings, and in many well-investigated cases of the past an assortment of panicky dogs, back-raised cats, and even vigilant rattlesnakes were involved. The following is an extract from an investigation of a haunted house in Kentucky made by Graham Watkins, now a research associate at the Psychical Research Foundation, in which a dog, cat, rat, and rattlesnake were introduced into the haunted room.

The dog upon being taken about two or three feet into the room immediately snarled at its owner and backed out the door. No amount of cajoling could prevent the dog from struggling to get out and refusing to reenter. The cat was brought into the room carried in the owner's arms. When the cat got a similar distance into the room, it immediately leaped upon the owner's shoulders, dug in, then leaped to the ground, orienting itself toward a chair. It spent several minutes hissing and spitting and staring at the unoccupied chair in a corner of the room until it was finally removed. Then a laboratory rat was brought in. The rat proceeded to move around peacefully and showed no apparent signs of disturbance at all . . .

Finally the rattlesnake was brought in and set in the center of the room in its little terrarium with glass walls. It immediately assumed an attack posture focussing on the same chair that had been of interest to the cat. After a couple of minutes it slowly moved its head toward the window, stopped, then moved back and receded into an alert posture five minutes later. When placed in another room of the house not linked with past tragedy, none of the four animals showed a noticeable response (*Theta*, nos. 33–34).

One of the oldest methods for investigating a haunting is with the use of a psychic. The sensitive is introduced into the house and asked to obtain impressions from it. Hopefully the psychic will be able to reveal information about the house which can later be verified. Unfortunately it is a moot point if this information really bears directly on the haunting, and the whole procedure depends on how much stock the investigator chooses to place in his psychic. More recently this method has been refined and elaborated by the use of several psychics. Each is allowed to tour the house. It is hoped that independently these psychics will describe either personality traits of the "ghost" or the areas it is most likely to haunt. Each report can then be compared to the impressions of the others or to the testimony of the family or other chief witnesses.

No one of these methods is any more conclusive than the others. It is very much up to the investigator himself to carry out a full inquiry, using his ability as an expert on what types of phenomena usually occur in a haunting, his competency in spotting inconsistencies in the reports, his skill in spotting motives or evidence of fraud, and his aptitude in evaluating the credibility of those he is interviewing. In short, it is a matter of experience.

The first three hauntings I investigated showed three different aspects of the pseudohaunting: a normal physical explanation, a psychological cause, and a good old-fashioned hoax. These cases illustrate the difficulties inherent in investigations of hauntings.

The first case was a follow-up to a phone call to the Southern California branch of the ASPR in 1968. Barbara Smith, the administrative assistant, took the call and the reporter described to her how he and others had become aware of rapping sounds in the bedroom of his large house in Pasadena. He was sure it was a ghost and by consulting with a local amateur psychic and through a Ouija board had determined that it was the spirit of a young child who had died in the house. The investigation was a melodramatic affair. Barbara, Raymond Bayless, and I were to meet at the house at midnight and hold vigil there for the psychic communication. We arrived at the hour designated and met the man who had called and were introduced to his two women companions. They were well imbued with wine—mixing their spirits it would seem. We sat in the rambling one-story-*avec*-basement house and after a while did hear a semirhythmic tapping coming from the floorboards. With the use of a stethoscope it wasn't hard to find the exact location of the tapping. These raps were hardly psychic—they were faint, rhythmic, and stationary which is not indicative of genuine phenomena. Raymond and I nodded to each other, confirming that we both knew exactly what the trouble was. We asked to be shown the basement and were escorted down a flight of stairs. There we found the hot water heater and showed our host the network of pipes under the house which led under the infested bedroom. We tapped the heater lightly and showed how the sound traveled down the pipes, causing raps to sound under the bedroom floor. All that was needed here was a plumber. The entire investigation lasted but half an hour. The residents made an abrupt about-face in their attitude toward the haunting and echoed that merry refrain, "Well, we really didn't think there was anything to it."

Physical explanations for hauntings are not always so easily detected. A startled man called reporting incredibly loud raps sounding like explosions which reverberated from the walls of his bedroom. The man was intelligent and sincere, which made the case sound promising, so Raymond and I scurried down to central Los Angles to investigate the matter. The caller turned out to be a very noble elderly Mexican gentleman who told us he had once fought as a lieutenant under Pancho Villa. He showed us around his small Spanish-style home accompanied by his pet chicken (!) which clucked affectionately around his feet. He told us that raps, pops, and explosions emanated from one wall in the late evenings. That was the catch; the raps always came from the same wall. So we waited and waited . . . and waited. As the evening wore on the temperature fell and the house became uncomfortably cold. The gentleman explained that the house had a gas heater that would activate automatically when the temperature fell below a certain degree. It was now obvious that the house had fallen well below a comfortable temperature, and it was evident that the gas heater was malfunctioning. It was probably the culprit of the haunting as well. Malfunctioning gas heaters are often the invoker of spirits. In this case it was apparent that as the heater attempted to activate gas escaped or leaked, setting up gas pockets. The heater was producing the horrendous racket, and it was from the adjoining bedroom wall that the raps were originating. We never actually heard the sounds, but we explained our suspicions to our host who promised to look into the matter. We must have been correct in our assumption since we never heard another word from him.

My next haunting had a psychological basis. Again, the investigation was made by Raymond and myself and centered on a middle-aged and very unhappy artist in a Hollywood apartment. Before we even entered his apartment we knew that the haunting offered only the tiniest hope of having any genuine aspects. But it was one of those reports you just can't pass up, for the man was claiming that a ghost was sexually molesting him! We drove into Hollywood and discussed the matter with him. He was genuinely sincere and claimed that for the past several nights, as he lay in bed, a female apparition appeared and exerted a "sexual influence" over him. He would feel drained and then the apparition would depart. In talking with the artist we soon uncovered a psychological cause of the situation. In middle age he was still a bachelor. He had had several romantic involvements but none had developed into marriage. Significantly, shortly before the apparition materialized his latest fiancée had broken off their engagement and he admitted being wracked by guilt and loneliness. His troubles had so plagued him that he had converted to a firm religious belief. It was clear that the apparition was a product of his own guilt and frustration. Since he was a religious man we suggested that religious rites be performed to alleviate the haunting. It must be pointed out that this suggestion was made years before the exorcism craze started, sparked by William Blatty's novel and the highly publicized motion picture based on it. We recommended that these rites be read over the apartment or himself because such rituals do have a beneficial psychological effect. The ritual is a placebo, since it works on the beliefs of the sufferer. It also represents to him a method of fighting magic by magic. Many psychologically based hauntings are "cured" in this way since the people involved expect them to be. Our host thought the idea was practical. (Of course we did not tell him why we suggested this course of action, nor that we felt the haunting was evoked by his own mind.) We left, urging him to call us if any further difficulties arose. He never did.

The last of my early investigations centered on a pretty, middle-class home in the San Fernando Valley occupied by a family that included two daughters and a much younger son. The house was reported as being haunted shortly after the wide publicity given the alleged haunting of the Elke Sommer-Joe Hyams home in Los Angeles, and like the latter was reported by a call to UCLA. The chief investigator there was Dr. Freda Morris who passed the report on to me. I drove out to the house and talked to the mother and both daughters. The father remained aloof from the whole matter. The occupants described an exciting array and a delicious feast of phenomena—bells ringing, objects flying about, beds bouncing up and down, and on and on. The curious feature of the haunting was that no two witnesses had ever observed the same incident. Each had his or her own stock of ghost stories which he or she was telling with great relish. It certainly seemed odd that with so many incidents taking place day in and day out, I was assured, that no *two* people could corroborate even one. It was very suspicious and I was fairly certain that a hoax was being perpetrated. All the facts pointed to it. In order to test my feelings about the case, I engaged the family members in a discussion during which I suggested perfectly ridiculous types of phenomena which I said often occur during hauntings, implying that they should have experienced them. The family fell right into the trap. They elaborated on my suggestions and made up wild reports in keeping with my suggestions but completely atypical of genuine hauntings. I have found this to be a chief aid when exploring such cases. The percipients are usually not well informed about hauntings, and their reports are often at variance with the types of encounters recorded in well-authenticated cases. (For example, "ghosts" are only very rarely heard to speak.) Usually these people will be tripped up by reporting something so out of the normal pattern that suspicion is justified. They want desperately to have their stories believed and will follow every suggestion proposed to make up a good ghost story. It is this incentive that leads them into the trap. I suggested types of phenomena that never occur during hauntings, and the family took the cue and claimed to have indeed encountered these very same effects. The haunting was one of those cases where you had to shovel through the lies to get to the front door.

More important than the worthlessness of the report is the question, why did they perpetrate the hoax? There are many dynamics that lead people to fake hauntings as will be shown later in this chapter, but in this particular case the mother wanted publicity. She had visions of herself as a psychic consultant and even the local comment had brought several neighbors eager to appreciate her advice as a psychic. The haunting took her away from the everyday quality of her life and added a spark of status, intrigue, and excitement to her life. It was inevitable that her two daughters should involve themselves with similar claims. The girls became celebrities at their high school, achieved greater social status by talking about the haunting, and even started to hold séances in the house. As for the father, he was oblivious to the whole thing, being either hoodwinked by his own family or, knowing that the whole thing was nonsense, preferred to retreat into silence at the risk of alienating them. What makes this case so sad is that several amateur parapsychologists, including a UCLA faculty member, were completely taken in by the report, and in consequence added encouragement to the family. Several years later I found this entire case written up very enthusiastically in a popular book on hauntings.

Both the author and the UCLA "specialist" had lacked one thing—the use of a little common sense.

Yet, beneath this weed garden of malobservation and fraud lie a few genuine hauntings. It is the search for these rare psychic outbreaks that prompts one to look into every single report, follow every lead, in the hope of stumbling across the paranormal. Sooner or later a genuine case arises. The Thomas haunting was just such a one and came to us through a typical call to the Southern California Society for Psychical Research. As in many such cases, the caller was referred to Raymond Bayless who phoned me immediately.

The Thomas household consisted of Mrs. Thomas, her mother, and a five-year-old daughter, all of whom had witnessed the phenomena. When Mrs. Thomas spoke to us, the events had been occurring for the past several weeks. The main phenomena consisted of voices calling the names of the family members. Mrs. Thomas reported to us how on several occasions, late at night she heard her name called gently. At first she thought it was her imagination until one day, after she had heard the voice, her daughter came to her asking, "Why don't you answer the man, Mommy?" The daughter was, as stated, only five years old and Mrs. Thomas wanted to keep her ignorant of the affair. Although she overheard some of our first interview, we did not talk with her or question her independently. Mrs. Thomas' mother vouched for the incidents and also claimed to have heard her name called by a male voice. We were told how, upon entering the living room on one occasion, Mrs. Thomas had seen at the table in the far corner of the dining area a whitish female figure which dissolved as she watched it. She also reported that household objects often had been found tipped over, but since the family includes two dogs and a cat, we preferred to believe that the animals were the gremlins responsible.

At the end of the first interview neither Raymond nor I had formed any definite opinion on the case. The Thomases did admit that they had a somewhat erratic alcoholic neighbor next door who in the past had thrown rocks at their house. It seemed reasonable to believe that he could have been responsible for playing a cruel practical joke. We left after counseling the family about what hauntings are: that they were harmless and they should not be afraid, and that the incidents would soon abate and die out. We tried to encourage them to keep their minds off whatever was happening and to stay active with hobbies or family activities. This is the type of sound advice we always give to frightened families whether or not we believe a genuine haunting is on the loose. This helps the family psychologically and reassures them. Mrs. Thomas and her mother struck us as very intelligent people, but quite disturbed about the incidents that were taking place.

We have found that in investigations such as this, the family just wants, more than anything else, to talk to someone. This need fulfilled, we rarely get follow-up calls. But Mrs. Thomas was different, and about two months later she phoned Raymond again reporting a new outbreak of incidents. We drove to the house and found a very upset woman. For the last few days there had been a rash of physical effects plaguing the house which came to a head on May 1.

Missy, my daughter, was watching a cartoon on T.V. in the bedroom. I was on the bed behind her, reading. Around 8:30 [P.M.] she turned around and asked me who it was that she heard calling me. I told her I had heard nothing. She repeated that someone was calling me from the hall or the bathroom and I had better go check. She insisted that someone was calling my name, and that the voice was male. We went together down the hall to the area in front of the bathroom door and she said the voice was coming from there. I told her she was just hearing an echo from next door. (The neighbors fight often and are quite noisy.) We then walked into the living room and stood just inside the door. My mother's Yashica camera was in the middle of the table. It raised itself off the table and threw itself at me. It landed at my feet and just sort of bounced. Then the door started slamming and the dogs started barking and crying. We went back into the bedroom and everything remained quiet for a length of time. Missy went to sleep. Around 9:30 the dogs started to howl again and I went to the front of the house to check. The door was slamming and bouncing on its hinges. The two dogs were aimed at the door and their hair was standing straight up, while they were barking. It was a business bark, so I opened the inside door to see who was there. The screen door just slammed in my face. I locked the inside door as fast as possible and ran like hell for the bedroom. Missy was still asleep and had not been bothered. The dogs barked and howled three more times during the night. These times I did not check. Around 12:30 I began to hear voices just sort of discussing something out of my hearing. Again I checked but there was nothing to be found. The house has a parking lot just outside the windows. Thinking it might have come from there I opened all the windows to see. Nothing was in the parking lot. It sounded like a large group of people murmuring quietly just out of earshot.

Mrs. Thomas was concerned that someone might be injured by the hurling objects, especially her young daughter. Again, by the time we arrived the incidents had abated. We assured the family that no harm would come to them and urged they call us immediately as soon as any ostensibly paranormal incidents occurred again.

It wasn't long until that chance came. Only a few weeks later Mrs. Thomas placed an almost frantic call to Raymond. Calling at 7:20 P.M. she reported that disturbances had started at 3:00 P.M. While working at a drafting board where she does commercial artwork, several of her tools began to move by themselves. She had placed all of them nervously back into her toolbox, and as she spoke to Raymond, she described how at that very moment a pencil was raising itself from the drafting board and was cavorting about. I was unavailable that evening so Raymond rushed over to the Thomas residence, arriving fifteen minutes after the call. Mrs. Thomas was terrified. She had sent her daughter out of the house to keep her from any involvement. She was so frightened, Raymond told me later, that her hands were shaking so badly that she could hardly pour a cup of coffee. She showed Raymond her drafting table scarred by several irregular lines which she said were caused by the drafting pencils sliding over the board inexplicably. At Raymond's request she had left several of her tools on the floor where they had fallen mysteriously so that Raymond could see them before Mrs. Thomas tidied up. After waiting a few minutes Raymond decided to leave the house since it is well known that during haunting outbreaks a phenomenon will occur as soon as all backs are turned. At 8:00 when he stepped out of the house for a few minutes, Mrs. Thomas was picking up the tools and placing them back in the toolbox.

Raymond returned in about seven minutes, and looking through the screen door he saw an odd sight. Mrs. Thomas was standing in the middle of the room with her tools, very delicate and expensive equipment, strewn pell-mell over the living room floor. She told Raymond that the box had overturned of its own accord and that all the tools had catapulted from it. It could have been possible for Mrs. Thomas to have maneuvered this herself even though it resulted in damaging expensive property, but when Raymond bent over to examine and help clear up the disarray, he found that all the tools and the toolbox were covered by a wet residue. How this residue came there is a mystery and it seems hard to believe that Mrs. Thomas was responsible. This same feature has been found in a few other haunting cases; however I am sure that Mrs. Thomas knew nothing about this fact. The peculiar wetness of the objects, conforming to a little-known pattern, leads me to believe that the case was authentic. Of course, this incident only augments the combined testimony of the three witnesses (if one includes the daughter) whom we had spoken to on previous occasions.

During our second interview with the Thomases, we had suggested that religious rites be performed inasmuch as the family was Roman Catholic. If nothing else this would benefit them psychologically. After Raymond's third visit this course of action was again suggested. At the present writing (July 1974) the Thomases have reported no further disturbances. However the haunting is still well within the range of possible activity, and it may be that future developments will throw more light on this perplexing case.

As can be seen, finding a haunted house is a mite easier than catching the ghost. Because haunting outbreaks are so sporadic and unpredictable, the evidence for them is usually restricted to the reports of the persons involved. Perhaps one or two friends or neighbors might also share in the odd events, and in that case their testimony adds weight to the investigation, but it is only rarely that the psychical researcher himself is able to witness the haunting at firsthand. During the early years of psychical research it was not unusual for investigators to rent a reputedly haunted house and either live in it or billet other investigators there for several weeks or even months.

I was able to do this between 1972–1974, living in a haunted house for a little over two years. During that time I interviewed several people who had lived there previously as well as recorded several incidents in which I participated myself. In a previous book, *An Experience of Phantoms*, I recounted several adventures in this house, but since that time new verification has come to light along with the discovery of the house's most unusual background.

The house was built in the 1920s. It is a little Spanish-style house in Canoga Park, California, that had been remodeled and an addition put on during the 1950s. The house has a rather peculiar floor plan. The front door opens directly into the living room and it in turn leads into a large den area. The den on one side leads into the kitchen-dining area and on the other side into an alcove separating the bathroom and the master bedroom. At the rear of the den is another door which originally led onto a back patio which had subsequently been enclosed and turned into a second bedroom. The three previous tenants who shared the house were friends of mine. They all had described how objects had disappeared, told of odd feelings while in the house, how objects shifted position when no one was home, and of hearing odd sounds at night. In December 1971 one of the tenants, Carlos Romero, was searching for someone with whom to share the house and expenses, and I jumped at the chance to move into the house later that month. However, I was preparing to leave on a trip so I didn't actually live in the house until January, when I was given the back bedroom.

The reported events had been rare and infrequent, and it was a long wait before anything precipitated in the house during my occupancy. The jolt came on April 16, one evening while I was out visiting. The next morning a startled Carlos told me of an inexplicable occurrence the night before. Around 9:30 P.M., while he was lying on his bed looking over some music, he heard the front screen door open, the wooden door open and shut, and then heard footsteps progress from the door across the wooden floor at a firm, steady pace. At first he merely assumed that I was coming home. However his Great Dane, a placid animal with a sweet disposition who *never* barked when I entered, or for that matter hardly ever barked at a stranger, began to react furiously. Carlos jumped from the bed and found the dog staring directly at the front door and barking in great agitation. Plainly no one was in sight and the front door was locked as usual.

The day before this incident I had been resting in my room when suddenly the bed jiggled under me. My first impression was that Carlos' cat had jumped on the bed, but then it dawned on me that I had put the cat outside earlier that day. I didn't think about the incident at all until Carlos told me of his adventure. For the next few days my bed was shaken on several occasions and sometimes the force would push on the foot of the bed. But once while I was fully awake and perfectly still, the top of the bed was given an almost staggering punch which I could literally feel right next to my head.

During this same period Carlos awoke one night to hear moaning and crying coming from the wall adjacent to his bed. This whole rash of events lasted but a few days. Probably the most striking was the response of the Great Dane.

Her furious barking was totally at odds with her normal habits. Many months later I witnessed some rather peculiar antics of the dog myself. I was sitting in the living room, alone in the house, when I noticed that the dog was staring intently from the den into my bedroom. I walked up behind her, but she took no heed of me but continued to stare and concentrate. After several moments of absolute stillness, she crouched down on her paws and proceeded to stalk something invisible across the den floor and into my room. The dog stared at the same point throughout, but after entering my room and sniffing about, seemed content, pranced out, and that was the end of the incident.

December 1973 brought with it more phenomena which began with my waking up to hear what sounded like violin strings being bowed randomly. The next day brought the climax to all the events I witnessed in the house. I thought Carlos was in the kitchen sweeping the floor and I called to him, "What else did she say?" That was a query about a phone call he had received earlier in the evening from a girl we knew. A gruff voice answered, "Nothing . . . nothing . . . nothing." It was a hoarse male whisper which I assumed was Carlos'. I walked into the kitchen to ask another question and found Carlos just entering the house through the back door. He had been outside in the yard all the while, had not heard me call to him and just then very hesitatingly reported that the night before he had heard a voice in *his* room.

During this entire time objects would mysteriously vanish. It was hard to isolate just when the disappearances took place, but every so often we would notice that our set of steak knives was suddenly depleted or that sheets were missing. This was not our imagination since two of the former tenants described similar events. Even though it was hard to determine the timing of these incidents, one was so overt that there could be no mistake about it. The disappearances followed a definite pattern. One of a kind objects never vanished. It was only when we had a group of similar items that one or more of them suddenly became unaccounted for. During June 1972 I had a throat infection which necessitated my taking tetracycline capsules. On June 24 I only had three left, and since the following evening I had an important social engagement, I decided to take only one on the twenty-fourth saving two for the next day. I carefully placed these two capsules back into the bottle. The next day to my astonishment only one capsule remained. No one had visited the house in the meantime and the disappearance had no apparent normal cause.

When I finished *An Experience of Phantoms* in April 1973, I mentioned in it that since December 1972 the house had been silent and that I did not expect any further phenomena for several months. The manifestations came in August in a very evidential manner. Earlier that summer I had left Los Angeles for Durham, North Carolina, to work at the Psychical Research Foundation. Since, by this time I was living in the house by myself and did not want to leave it unattended for the six weeks I would be gone, I asked a friend of mine to stay there during my absence. He actually remained until January when he left for Berkeley when the house was sold and I had to move. Just before moving I mentioned several things to him about the house and told him that I had said nothing before as it would have reduced the value of any evidence he might submit had he encountered any manifestations there. He became very upset and did report something odd. Many times during my absence he heard thumping in the house at night. Each time he got up to investigate and each time nothing could be found. These loud but dull thuds seemed to come from the living room. He had been puzzled by them but not disturbed. (Later that night I came home to find him on the phone nervously explaining to a friend that he was afraid to spend any more nights in the house.)

The end of the investigation came in January 1974 when I had to move out of the house. I had always been reluctant about discussing these encounters with the owners of the house, but once I had left I did call them to ask if they had ever heard or seen anything unusual while they lived there. They had lived in the house for ten years and were very surprised by my reports. They denied having any psychic confrontations during their residency. From 1958 until the present they had often rented it but none of the tenants had ever complained. (This, though, is meaningless since I doubt if many tenants would complain to their landlord that a house was haunted. Further, they may well have overlooked or rationalized away any supernormal outbreaks.)

My hopes of finding a specific cause for the haunting was never satisfactorily realized. However, a possible key to the mystery did come to light during my investigation of the house's early history. It had been originally owned by a Protestant minister who had lived there for several years and during that time his wife had died, although not in the house. While there he had turned the large den into a wedding chapel and many marriages had taken place in the house. Could it be that we were picking up the residue from the strong emotions linked with the chapel?

This final testimony concerning my little haunted house was not the only haunting activity that came to light in my absence that summer. Another haunting was rampaging in an apartment in Van Nuys, California.

On August 13, 1973, Raymond Bayless was called in to investigate a haunting centering on the residence of Mr. and Mrs. Ceccato and their four-year-old daughter. When I returned from Durham a few weeks later, I joined in the investigation. Mrs. Ceccato was very fearful of the poundings and telekinesis she had witnessed, and after telling Raymond of their experiences, both the Ceccatos agreed that they would be willing even to take a lie-detector examination to prove the truth of their testimony. Mr. Ceccato, age twenty-eight, had encountered these same manifestations in several other houses in which he had lived. Taking these similar incidents into account the entire case spans over fifteen years.

As a child Mr. Ceccato remembered hearing poundings and mysterious footsteps in his parents' home, and at fifteen he had written a short story incorporating his own experiences. One time he and his brother heard footsteps on the roof of the house, and when they ran out to check they saw roof pebbles move and slide off the roof even though there was no wind blowing and nothing was in sight.

When the Ceccatos moved to Los Angeles, the "family ghost" moved with them, and they recorded similar sounds of footsteps in their several residences. During a year's stay in their first Van Nuys home, they noted telekinetic movement of objects, pictures rotating on the walls, and knockings at the front door as well as inside the house. However the incidents that finally persuaded the

Ceccatos to call in psychical investigators began in July 1973. As Mr. Ceccato wrote in his account that we asked him to submit:

On several occasions loud poundings apparently coming from an insulated attic were heard. A knife that had been placed on an end table to the left of the sofa had been mysteriously moved to a coffee table in front of and centered with the sofa—a distance of nearly 4½ feet.

On two occasions knocking was heard on the front door and when the door was opened no one was there. The first noticeable incident exhibiting what might be termed a "violent nature" occurred at about 6:30 P.M. July 25, 1973. The incident was witnessed by three members of our family while sitting at dinner at the kitchen table nearly twelve feet from the occurrence. A candle almost one foot in height and solidly placed in a gold plated glass candle holder with a base measuring three inches from the wall to the edge of the mantle. The candle holder was against the wall when for no apparent reason and with no visible outside force the candle and holder were thrust off the mantle flying three feet away from the wall onto the floor and breaking.

After this incident many household items began to disappear mysteriously, and all the while the violent nature of the phenomena continued as the following handwritten statement by Mrs. Ceccato avers:

July 28. About 4:30 P.M. I was vacuuming the living room. I had caught out of the corner of my eye a coffee table in front of the sofa just coming down and hitting the floor. 'Someone' had evidently picked it up, turned it around and sat it down again. When I saw the table with both eyes and facing it, it was nearly 2½–3 inches off the ground.

In August of that summer more phenomena erupted, including wild poundings on the wall and the teleportation of an ashtray. This latter incident was especially well witnessed by the family and their guests while sitting in the living room. Mr. Ceccato's sister had brought in an ashtray and set it on the coffee table for all to use. Just a few moments later one of the guests lit a cigarette, tried to dispose of the burned match, but the ashtray had vanished. Everyone searched for it, eventually discovering it in the kitchen—a room no one had entered during the get-together.

It was just after this incident that we entered the case. As with the Thomas case, there was little to do at this point except to interview all available witnesses. The Ceccatos were in no way reticent about putting us in touch with their friends and relatives who had witnessed these outbreaks, and we were able to speak with them to determine if they would verify or deny the Ceccatos' story. There were no inconsistencies.*

Although the phenomena were active during our investigation, we had not so far been able to witness any of the events ourselves. But, armed with a tape recorder, Mr. Ceccato was able eventually to record the poundings that plagued the house. These rappings were the most frightening of all the phenomena they had observed. Here is a typical account given to us by Mrs. Ceccato on tape:

> I was in the bathroom combing my hair and Angel [their daughter] kept calling me. She was standing at the threshold of the kitchen. She kept calling me to come; I was hurrying and was a little bit amazed at the time but I came in to answer her. She said "Listen to noise" pointing into the kitchen. I was standing at the kitchen door on the outside and I couldn't hear a thing. I stepped into the kitchen and there was a horrible pounding that was shaking the lamp in the kitchen. Not this one on the dining room table but the one in the kitchen. And yet you step back into the hallway and nothing. Not one sound.

The fact that the poundings did not obey acoustical laws is in itself evidence of the paranormality of the noise. It was impossible to produce any noise in the kitchen that would not be heard in the adjoining hallway since the living room, kitchen, and hall are all very compact. It would seem that the noise had its own "sphere of influence," and one could only hear the sounds when that sphere was entered. Such quirks are not rare in hauntings. Horrendous crashes of smashing crockery might be heard, yet everything will be found in perfect order upon investigation. Furniture may be heard shifting about in a room which when entered is found to be untouched.

* One witness described for us how while baby-sitting she had heard knockings on the front door. She had peered out the window next to the door and although she continued to hear the knocks saw no one there.

The Ceccatos' poundings fall into this same pattern since the noises and physical effects were partitioned off.

Some years previously Mr. Ceccato had tape-recorded the footsteps he has heard all his life in the various homes he occupied, but had lost the tape. The upsurge of the present incidents encouraged him to try again to record the odd noises that were becoming increasingly common. This opportunity came on September 20. Mr. Ceccato was the sole witness but wrote a statement signed by himself, his wife, and sister who heard the tape immediately after he had made the recording. Mr. Ceccato was extremely excited and nervous but swore "as God is my witness" that he was telling the truth. Before describing the bizarre tape recording, here is Mr. Ceccato's account:

> About 5:20 P.M. I was lying in the bathtub. I was practically sound asleep. I heard what sounded like a loud muffled voice over a loud speaker. I could not understand the voice, if it was in fact a voice. There was a distinct echo in the tone. It startled me out of my sleep.
>
> I leaped out of the tub, wrapped a towel around myself and ran into the living room. I looked in front of the house to see if there was any sign of a public announcement system or systems. There was no such sign. I went into the backyard to look for the same thing. I found nothing. I heard no children or cars in the area. The sound lasted only a couple of seconds.
>
> I started back to the bathroom to dry off. As I started to walk through the hall I heard the familiar poundings on the walls and the rattling of the ceramic pictures on the wall. I stopped in the hall to listen. In ten seconds the pounding had stopped. I told myself I was going to record the sounds if it killed me.
>
> It took about four minutes to get and set up my tape recorder. I put the recorder on the laundry hamper in the guest bathroom. I put the mike on the floor, turned the volume all the way up, and turned the recorder on. I went to the door of my bedroom, stood at the threshold and stared at the recorder across the hall waiting for something to happen. Less than one minute later the pounding started. It's now about 5:30 P.M. After the pounding on the wall, I heard and recorded fourteen sounds that represented footsteps.

Mr. Ceccato's statement concludes with his account of playing the tape for his wife and sister who arrived home shortly after, with his assertion that the raps were identical to those heard by the Ceccatos in their previous domiciles.

The tape itself lasts only about forty seconds. It begins with a terrible din of quick rappings and rattling, percussive sounds which represent the violent jiggling of ceramic pictures on the wall. After a few seconds of silence come a series of fourteen incredibly loud blows. These sound like a sledgehammer pounding the floor. The "footsteps" are rhythmic and occur every two seconds or shortly before. After each blow an echo-like dull thud can be heard. No plumbing problems could possibly account for these noises. Any type of earth tremor or geological anomaly that could cause the sounds would have to be so severe as to tear the house from its foundation.

During the course of this investigation we were able to interview a number of witnesses, including Mr. Ceccato's sister and his mother who verified many of the incidents reported during her son's childhood. All told, the case is most impressive and the combined testimony indicates that the Ceccatos are the center of some very strange phenomena. (I say "are" because the case is still active and under our surveillance.) The most unusual feature of the case is its longevity, although after these events the phenomena slackened, and as of July 1974 the Ceccatos have reported very little psychic activity.

There are two types of hauntings: conventional hauntings and poltergeists. Conventional hauntings are long-drawn-out affairs which center on a specific place, be it a home, apartment, theater, and so on. During the course of the haunting many tenants will record the same phenomena which seem stationary and linked to one locale. On the other hand, a poltergeist is extremely violent, short-lived, and haunts a person not a place and can follow the agent even if he moves. In the Ceccato case we find a mixture of both types of hauntings. The actual phenomena are typical of the poltergeist: raps, objects moving, even the odd pebble movements on the roof he saw as a child. However poltergeist hauntings rarely last more than a few weeks, at the most a few months. Yet the Ceccato case has been active for many years. Like a haunting it is intermittent; outbreaks of incidents are followed by a long period of calm which in this case has extended up to several years. Yet the haunting has changed residences which is unheard of in traditional haunted houses. Poltergeists also usually center on a psychologically disturbed or frustrated member of the household. This pattern is totally lacking in the Ceccato case. This case has incorporated features from both the poltergeist and the conventional haunted house and this peculiarity makes it a double enigma.

If investigating a haunting is basically a waiting game, the conventional poltergeist is the exact opposite. Often things happen so suddenly, quickly, and frequently that it is nearly impossible to keep track of everything being overturned, broken, or thrown across a room. Now, not all cases are quite so dramatic, but some poltergeists consist of a barrage of incidents, one after the other, and it becomes impossible for any one person to keep track of everything. Sometimes the poltergeist victims make use of the confusion to throw about some objects themselves to add to the mystery. Investigating the poltergeist can be frustrating, as in the following case.

A family complained to the Southern California Society for Psychical Research that their home was the scene of violent bangings, objects being thrown, and other poltergeistic antics. The call was turned over to another colleague of mine who called me immediately. We ultimately spent two days at the house trying to keep a record of all that took place and to calm down the family at the same time. The family consisted of a teen-age girl, her mother, and an aunt. Actually, although during our stay over thirty incidents occurred, from bottles thrown, to rapping sounds on the walls, to furniture toppling over, it became almost impossible for the two of us to keep track of everything. The main problem was that we two investigators had to watch three people. This in itself would not have been too bad, but every time anything happened, all three members of the family would run about the house in panic as we tried to ascertain what had been thrown, where everyone was at the time of the incident, and if anyone could have thrown it normally.

Notwithstanding these difficulties, we were able to make two observations that seemed to indicate a genuine poltergeist was rampant. The first incident was observed only by me. It was early evening and no poltergeistery had disturbed the family for several hours. The focal point of the poltergeist, the teen-age girl, was sitting directly in front of me, her back propped against a wall. To the side of her stood her mother at the hallway entrance. The aunt was sitting next to me on a couch. The entire family was therefore under control, and at the fateful moment I could see every member of the family in the house. I was talking to the mother when all of a sudden a tremendous blow resounded from the hallway. My first impression was that someone had hit the wall with a sledgehammer. All the family members were terrified by the sound. I bolted into the hallway to see what, if anything, had caused the crash. I could hear that the sound emanated from the middle of the hallway. Right across from the bathroom door lay a little plastic compact that had not been there during my constant patrolling of the hall. It was this little object that had been thrown, although the object itself could not possibly have caused the horrendous crash. The compact was not even chipped and lay flat against the wall. If it had been thrown with any force, it would have been smashed to bits. But such is the oddity of the poltergeist, for the noise made was completely out of proportion to the size and weight of the object hurled. The crash was one of the most impressive things I've ever encountered in any investigation.

The other incident occurred the next day. The girl was sitting in a chair cater-cornered to the couch where I was seated, and my colleague was in the hall guarding the door to the back room where the two older women were. Again everyone was under control. Suddenly we both heard a pinging sound, and looking up I watched a spoon bounce off the hall door right in front of me and rebound into the living room. The girl could not have thrown it since I was with her in the living room and any movement by her would have been detected. At the actual time of the incident the girl was in my peripheral vision, and the spoon would have had to move past my line of vision if she had thrown it. And her mother and her aunt were in a distant room. It was also a very impressive incident.

Unfortunately these two incidents were just about the only certain ones we could verify during the course of the case. After the spoon incident the poltergeist seemed to abate, so after trying to help the family adjust to their experience, we too had to make our exit. This case, which I have so briefly summarized, aptly reveals how psychic phenomena can be so close at hand, yet so elusive and distant at the same time.

If you were to stumble upon a haunting, how should you handle it? This is one of the questions psychical researchers are most often asked. The answer is both simple and complicated. The simple answer is to determine whether it is genuine or fraudulent, but, as in the words of Hamlet, there's the rub. It is this determination that is difficult, and in the next few pages I would like to outline some hints on handling a reported haunting.

First, one should be aware of the basic types of psychic occurrences which most often manifest in a haunted house. These would include apparitions or apparitional forms, unaccountable cold feelings and sensations of being touched or being in the presence of something real but intangible, lights, voices, and other noises such as footsteps or rappings, movement of objects, or even unaccountable odors.

In order to analyze any encounters with these phenomena, accurate accounts should be immediately taken from *all* witnesses present or as soon as possible after each incident. Any observer to the haunting or to a specific incident should be interviewed separately so that no witness will be influenced by what another may say. These independent testimonies then can be checked either for mutual corroboration or for discrepancies. It is best for all the accounts to be written out instead of taken orally in order to ensure accuracy and so that a file can be made on the case. The investigator should be able to make a visit to the haunted premises to see for himself the actual layout of the home. This would also permit an investigation of the premises to check for two very important features: (1) any source that would prove a normal explanation for the incidents, including bad plumbing, leaks, damaged floorboards, and even reflections passing as ghosts, all of which can suggestion a family into thinking they are infested by a haunting; (2) to check the position of any members of the household present during each incident. In this way a preliminary assessment can be made on the possibility that the incident was deliberately manufactured. If, for example, one individual always seems unaccounted for on each occasion that an incident occurred, then this should arouse justifiable suspicion that there may be a human cause for the haunting. During any investigation the researcher should keep all the household members under strict surveillance during his visit. By doing this, he will be in the best possible position to determine whether an incident is genuine should anything paranormal occur in his presence.

These few general rules are in no way complete but will give some valid guidelines to use when making an amateur investigation of a haunted house. The second group of principles concerns what to look for in order to determine fraud. If the combined testimony of the witnesses does not add up to mutual corroboration, this is the first indication of a hoax. It is not necessarily proof of it since people often make errors when they rely on their memories. However, if the accounts do not match, and no one incident was ever witnessed by more than one witness, this too is suspicious. One should also be on the lookout for a possible "agent" who is manufacturing the haunting. These people often unmask themselves by (1) recording a proliferation of psychic encounters while the other household members report very few incidents or are just peripheral witnesses to the haunting: (2) being overenthusiastic about the events, showing a lack of fright or concern, and trying to influence the investigators; (3) making up exaggerated and out-of-pattern stories about the phenomena witnessed. Often, as in one case I outlined, they will exaggerate and improvise upon any leading information offered them by the investigator.

What are the motives for fraud? Motives change over the years. Twenty years ago, believe it or not, many hauntings were invented to get rent reductions or to break leases. In fact there is a very touchy legal question concerning haunted houses, and some years ago a six-hundred-page book was written in Italy on the law, rent, and tenancy vs. haunted houses. However today's reasons are usually social. Since there is so much publicity attached to the occult, people fake hauntings for that sake, for social advance, for excitement. One woman called asking me to check into her "haunted house." I said I would but told her that I wanted to interview the entire family including the two young children. The woman then suggested that since she had so much experience with her own haunted house I should take her out on my investigations. She was a member of several amateur psychic groups and was promoting her own home as haunted in order to get a social connection with Los Angeles' parapsychological elite. My suspicions were justified when I discovered that she had talked to several other investigators about her home as well. When the day arrived that I was to start the investigation, the woman called me and made some feeble excuse for not keeping her appointment, and never called back. I expected this for several reasons. The woman wanted to talk about her ghost, not exorcise it, and she certainly did not want a scientific investigation that might cast doubt on her stories. When a witness is more interested in talking than getting to the root of the problem, this is a sure sign of a hoax.

By far, though, children are the worst offenders when it comes to fake hauntings. Hiding behind the stereotyped innocence we bestow upon them, children can be about the most vicious sneaks when it comes to humbugging their friends and parents. Their resourcefulness is frequently formidable and their imaginations virtually endless. The following case is typical.

I was called in to investigate a wealthy family's home in the San Fernando Valley. The Crosby family consisted of the parents and their three children, the youngest being twelve. Several times the living room lights were found mysteriously lit after they had been turned off. When the family was downstairs, they heard noises upstairs, and vice versa. As I recorded each incident I noted that their twelve-year-old boy was never accounted for while most of the other family members were huddled together in one part of the two-story house. It seemed clear to me that the youngster was manufacturing the incidents by traipsing up and down the stairs, always giving the impression that he was upstairs or downstairs when any "paranormal event" occurred in some other part of the house. These suspicions were confirmed as I watched the family interaction that evening. The twelve-year-old boy was obviously in open competition with his older siblings for parental attention. He was a show-off and an attention seeker. This is a typical pattern found with children who fake hauntings. They want to be noticed and when they don't get attention normally, devise a haunting. Usually the parents also follow a pattern: they either are active in amateur psychic groups or have read popular books on the subject. Their interest in the occult becomes common family knowledge and the source of family discussions. The discussions actually feed the children with the requisite information they need about psychic happenings and give them the knowledge to begin the haunting. So in this case the pattern would be as follows: a family with an amateur enthusiasm for the psychic and the presence of young children, one of whom obviously wants attention. This pattern is so often encountered that it has become a classical situation leading to a hoax. In the Crosby case, the twelve-year-old even organized a séance for me. Actually, the very fact that a family has had some interest in the psychic *before* the haunting outbreak is very suspicious.

If children are found faking what does the investigator do? The answer is not easy at all. You cannot simply tell the parents that they are naïve dupes and that their children are cheats. Usually the adults want a cessation of the "haunting" and care little for any explanation. It is best to encourage the parents to ignore the incidents. Usually a haunting grows because the children find themselves the center of excitement and commotion, and this leads them to fake ever harder and more convincingly. In these cases I suggest that the parents not only ignore the events, but that they not even discuss psychic matters at all, keep the children from involving themselves with Ouijas and the like, and keep them actively engrossed in other activities. The parents can be told that these outbreaks are short-lived, that they usually burn out quickly, and that to give attention to the incidents might aggravate the situation. This is really not at all true; what in fact happens is simple. The children no longer find the haunting is fun since all their gratification is taken from them. Instead of getting the attention they want, they are ignored, and soon the haunting becomes a bore and dies away. And no one is any wiser that it was a hoax from the start.

On the other hand one might wish to voice his suspicions to the parents if, during the interview, the investigator thinks they can handle it.

What if it is the parents who are the hoaxers? Adults fake hauntings for publicity, for prestige, from boredom, or even to cover up a crime. Once I was involved in a "poltergeist" case in which one member of a group of young people living together was hit over the head with a table by a rival, which was blamed on a haunting. The whole haunting was manufactured to cover up the incident that landed one young man in the hospital with a concussion. The best bet with adults is to stop the investigation after the first interview and quietly withdraw, telling them that since the incidents are sporadic nothing much can be done until the haunting becomes active again. Suggest that they call you when more outbreaks disrupt the house, and I can assure you that they will not call back. In my experience only rarely has anyone faked an incident in my actual presence. Oftentimes during genuine hauntings, children especially might feel disappointed that nothing has happened during the investigator's stay, and they might try banging on walls in order to impress him. Raymond Bayless once investigated a poltergeist on the rampage. While undoubtedly genuine, a boy in the household began pounding on the walls in order to imitate the raps the poltergeist had made. He did this to increase the attention he had received when the genuine phenomena broke loose. He was quickly detected.* As the genuine rappings subsided, the boy's fraudulent activities increased to keep interest in the haunting alive. The investigator must be on the alert for these mixed cases. Many times hauntings are a mixture of both the genuine and the contrived.

As the reader can see, checking into a report on a haunting is more difficult than it looks. If anything, the golden rule for the investigator should be the law of pattern and consistency. As pointed out constantly in this chapter, paranormal phenomena do conform to general principles. It is the duty of the investigator to know these patterns and to compare each incident and the overall reports in a case under his attention to the classical hauntings verified in the past. It is more than likely that the family involved will not have a very academic background on the subject, and that being so they will usually report very conventional and consistent incidents if they are truthful, or exaggerated, exotic, or out-of-pattern incidents if they are lying. But unless the investigator himself is versed in the rich literature of hauntings and psychical research, his prowess as an observer will be limited and he will probably do more harm than good.

There is also the problem of where a stricken family or amateur inquirer can find a qualified investigator to take charge of the case. Unfortunately there are many books on the market by popular writers who claim to be psychical investigators. These books and their authors should not be taken seriously since usually the latter

* Raymond Bayless and Henry Gilroy, "Thumping Bumping Poltergeist in California" (*Fate*, May 1966).

are on the lookout for a good story more than they are in carrying out an investigation or helping the family involved. However, many people read these books and put faith in the authors. There are, it is sad to say, a great many pseudoparapsychologists running about claiming to be able to investigate properly all sorts of psychic happenings.

To ensure protection, a family trying to locate a qualified expert should contact a reputable parapsychological organization (and not an amateur one) or, although many times this is a poor substitute, a local college or university which might have either a faculty member interested in the field or has a person on file for you to talk to.

No matter how you are placed in contact with an investigator, the following queries should be made. (1) Is he a member of the Parapsychological Association? Most serious parapsychologists are members of the PA and can only be elevated to this body by showing an expertise in psychical research. Usually they are required to have graduate degrees, preferably a doctorate, and to have major scientific parapsychological publications to their credit. (2) Has the investigator published in a recognized parapsychological journal? Many pop "parapsychologists" have written popular-level books, but there are very tightly edited professional journals in which most recognized parapsychologists have been published. (3) What professional affiliations does he have? Most parapsychologists also have a connection with a professional group or hold academic positions. If none of these qualifications are met, then one should be suspicious of the investigator. These rules are not rigid and are only very general guidelines.

With these principles in mind, one can see that coming to grips with a genuine haunting poses formidable difficulties.

# 4

# Evenings in the Dark

Throughout the history of psychical research are reports of mediums during whose séances tables levitated, ghostly forms appeared, and cold breezes uncannily manifested. Despite these fanciful descriptions some of these mediums were tested by the greatest savants of their era. Eusapia Palladino, for instance, a semi-illiterate Italian medium whose major phenomena consisted of table levitations, objects moving by themselves, and so on, was tested by no less legendary scientists than Sir Oliver Lodge, the Nobel Prize–winning physiologist Charles Richet, and the famous father of criminology, Cesare Lombroso. All certified her genuineness. Other scientists, Mme Marie Curie, for example, were left in consternation. Testimony was taken about these rare mediums, experiments carried out, special laboratories were built, and photographs obtained—all pointing to the irrefutable evidence that there exists a physical psychic energy that on rare occasions or with rare individuals can manifest beyond the limits of the body. When this ability, psychokinesis, can be controlled we have a Palladino. If the force is uncontrolled, we witness the vicious destructiveness of the poltergeist. In any event "mind over matter" is no myth.

That the human organism houses some form of nonphysical energy that can move objects without physical contact or break apart physical matter is well documented. But it is a rarer ability than ESP, even though most gifted ESP subjects also have psychokinesis. The search for PK phenomena for several reasons has not been as avidly pursued by parapsychologists as ESP. PK phenomena are hard to control, sporadic, rare, more controversial, and more important, they are easily imitated.

It is this last issue which is the most problematic. During the history of psychical research there have been several gifted subjects who have claimed the PK ability, Eusapia Palladino being a case in point. But many times these individuals were caught ruthlessly faking their results. Often the experimenters themselves would be taken in by the fraud, but other times the physical phenomena were undoubtedly real. Differentiation between them became so difficult that the constant controversy about physical phenomena began to affect parapsychology's scientific respectability. Since séances for physical phenomena most often take place in the dark, both fraud and malobservation join in an unholy alliance. Take a table levitation, for example. People sit around a table in a darkened room. The table rocks backward and forward and finally levitates a few inches off the floor. What could be simpler to check and verify? This is not the case however. There are too many ways to fake this effect. One could pound a nail into the side of the table and levitate it by wearing a loosely fitted ring to insert over the nail during the experiment. One can slip a foot under one leg or use a hook around the waist to lift the table. If the lights are out and the hands are being held, it is easy to levitate a table with the back of the neck put down and under it. And these are only the more common ways.

Table tipping is one type of psychic practice that is very popular and most of the time very fraudulent. Just about everyone interested in the psychic field has seen or participated in table tipping. A group of people seat themselves around a light wooden or card table, placing their hands on it lightly. Soon the table begins to rock gently, finally wiggles around and begins to rock to and fro, popping up on one leg or two, and so forth. These movements are very impressive but hardly paranormal. The principle behind it is similar to that behind the Oiuja board. No one consciously pushes the Oiuja, but it is done by subconscious involuntary movements of the hand. During table tippings all the sitters actually begin to push and shove unconsciously, eventually exerting so much force that the table will move and even spring about erratically. But it is nothing more than the motions of the sitters all oblivious to the fact that they are causing them. This principle was proved by none other than Michael Faraday who invented a device that would monitor involuntary hand motions. When Faraday's gauge was installed (a type of circular false table top), while it moved, the table underneath did not. Another method to stop muscular movements during table tipping is spreading cold cream over the table top. Cold cream is so slick that no one can get leverage and the fingers, even if moved minutely, glide over the cream, leaving an incriminating path.

Fraud can be conscious or unconscious. I attended a series of table-tilting sessions with two women "mediums" who were promoting themselves as table tilters. The lights were dimmed but not turned out and sure enough after a little while bounce went the table. By watching one of the mediums it was easy to discern that when the table tilted, the color of her fingernails whitened, showing that she was quite consciously putting pressure on the tips of her fingers, deliberately causing the table movements. Since I was right next to the medium, I merely worked my leverage against hers so that I, not she, could maneuver the table. Whenever she tried to push it, I made sure the table didn't budge. When she stopped trying, I then would give the table a little shove. This game went on for quite some time until the medium began to show great consternation over the situation.

Reading these comments one might wonder at the blatancy of the fraud. Yet, as a matter of fact, just about everyone at the séance had not only fallen for the display, but also felt that we were in contact with the world unseen. One woman became hysterical, pounded the table and screamed, thinking her dead mother was communicating and trying to kill her sister. I have seen this type of hysterical paroxysm and frenzy several times in the course of fraudulent séances. But all physical phenomena are not so easily dismissed as fraud.

What opened a new chapter in my search for the psychic began in 1969 due to a chance meeting with Dr. Robin Sanders-Clarke. Robin was in his fifties and had been a council member of the long defunct British College of Psychic Science founded in 1920 by the Spiritualist, J. Hewat MacKenzie. (The BCPS has no relation to the College of Psychic Studies now active in Great Britain.) The BCPS had been a clearing house for mediums and the roster of their staff psychics was spectacular. It included, among others, Eileen Garrett who later became one of today's most well-known mediums. It also sponsored Arthur Ford, another stellar psychic. Meeting Robin was like opening a gate into the rich history of psychical research. He had had an incredible amount of experience with mediums, knew the ins and outs of fraud, and was eager to get actively involved in experimentation again. This led to the development of a "home circle" in which a group of us experimented regularly, trying to induce, witness, and verify physical phenomena.

Before chronicling the encounters with the unseen these experiments provided, a little background on what a home circle is and how it worked should be given. Spiritualism was launched as a religious movement in 1848 when a series of raps haunted a little house owned by the Fox family in Hydesville, New York. It was soon discovered that these raps could communicate intelligently and claimed to be communications from the dead. Whether or not the Rochester rappings, as they became known, were genuine or bogus is still debated today. Nonetheless the revelation that man could encounter the dead became the basis for a cult that soon spread throughout the United States and Great Britain. Every family who belonged to the cult began home experimentations, usually with table turning which became a very fashionable practice in this country and among the middle classes in Great Britain and France. It was thought, of course, that spirits directed the dancing tables and codes were devised by which to talk with them. Questions were asked and answered by the table which tilted a certain number of times for yes and a certain number of times for no. The table could even spell out messages by tipping when a specific letter was called.

Gifted mediums were aplenty, again real and fake, with the latter far outnumbering the former. However one of the main tenets of Spiritualism was that a family could communicate with the dead even in the absence of a talented medium. This lead to the concept of the home circle. It was believed that if a group sat diligently week after week in a darkened room, sitting around a table or merely as a group, very gradually enough "power" would develop and physical phenomena would eventually occur, or that one member of the group would develop mediumship.

This may seem very naïve, but there is rich testimony that home circles can evolve into an excellent breeding ground for psychic phenomena. During the 1920s and 1930s many popular books were written by people who developed home circles within their own families. Books such as *Death's Door Ajar*, *The Consoling Angel*, and others recounting experiences in private circles were very popular in Great Britain. Other notable Spiritualists such as Hannen Swaffer and Maurice Barbanell openly testified to their own psychic encounters in these groups. Even Hereward Carrington, one of psychical research's most critical investigators, admitted that one of the most phenomenal displays of physical phenomena he had ever observed took place in a home circle.

It was with all this in mind that Raymond Bayless and I enthusiastically welcomed Robin Sanders-Clarke's suggestion that we form a small group for the purpose of sitting regularly to see if we actually could develop physical phenomena. Robin had much experience in this area, so in January 1969 we began a long series of evenings in the dark.

For the experiments a small group of close friends formed the nucleus: Raymond and his wife, Marjorie, Robin, myself, my mother, Winifred Rogo, and two other sitters who will be identified by their initials: A.G., a clinical psychologist, and G.L., a secretary. The plan for the sittings was simple but rigid. Each week we would meet at the same place and at the same time. We all vowed to attend regularly, only missing in cases of dire necessity. (According to Spiritualist manuals, the only acceptable reasons for absence are illness and summer vacation.) To achieve this end, we converted Raymond's small study into the séance room. When not in use, this room was closed off. In order to sit we procured metal folding chairs set tightly in a circle, almost touching each other. The room was completely blacked out. In this way no one could move about since any movement would cause the sitter to bump into the person next to him, and any overt action could easily be detected by the rest of the group. If anyone moved or otherwise created any noise, he or she immediately called it for the records. We sat around an old-fashioned tin speaking trumpet, hoping that eventually it would move, or be tapped loudly, or generally be the focus for any telekinetic effects that might occur. My mother developed a method of writing in the dark and kept precise records of all events.

The formal structure of the sittings followed conventional Spiritualist home circle procedures. The reason for adopting them was based on several rationales: (1) they were traditional; (2) others had followed them and claimed success with them; (3) they structuralized the experiments; (4) Robin had used these methods before with good results. The principles were simple. We would engage in some friendly socializing before the sitting and then would adjoin to the sitting room. All lights would be extinguished, and windows and doors sealed. A greeting would be given, and for the next hour we would occasionally and sparingly chat or play background music on a cassette. After about an hour or an hour and a half we would close the sitting and the experiment was over for the night. According to home circle tradition, this is a slow process, and some circles reported waits of up to two years before anything took place. With this in mind we began a series of fifty-two sittings.

The patience to which we had committed ourselves was tested from the beginning. For ten straight weeks absolutely nothing occurred, but on the tenth sitting we had our first evidence that we might be able to record physical phenomena. As usual we began the sitting at about 7:00 P.M. About forty-five minutes later Marjorie reported that something had brushed against her. A.G., who sat next to her, had not moved.

Our optimism was well justified, for at our eleventh sitting we had several minor phenomena. Twenty minutes after we began, Marjorie again reported that something had touched her shoe. For the next half hour many of us heard tiny rappings. This type of gentle clicking sound had never been heard before in our almost three months of experiments. During this series of clickings, which lasted intermittently for about twenty minutes, two loud raps, as though made on wood, were heard. I should note that I am very familiar with the Bayless home, having been a frequent guest over the two years prior to the experiments and knew very well the sound of the house settling and its thermal creaks. The weather outside was clear and cool with no unusual atmospheric conditions that might affect a house.

The next two sittings were blanks. It was as though the power that had activated itself before was now in the process of conserving itself. One odd phenomenon did occur though. During the twelfth sitting we all heard a loud whistle with the exception of A.G. It sounded like someone exhaling air forcibly between the teeth and from the nose. We immediately suspected that A.G. had unconsciously made the noise since he did not hear it, but this he emphatically denied.

With the blank sitting behind us, the April 7 sitting was the most impressive we had had to date. Fifteen minutes after the séance commenced, G.L. reported she had been touched on her finger. Fifteen minutes after that a loud rap was heard from behind the circle which sounded as though someone had rapped knuckles on Raymond's desk. Fifteen minutes later Robin reported his first touch, a quick brush on his leg. So far the phenomena had been occurring in patterns of every fifteen minutes and lasted that way throughout the evening. Fifteen minutes later another strong and loud rap was heard by the group, followed by Robin again reporting a touch, this time on his ankle.

As with the previous sittings, this outbreak of manifestations put a damper on the ability of the telekinesis to perform, and although we recorded very light raps, nothing substantial happened the following two weeks. But again, the very next sitting offered some new and striking phenomena. According to home circle tradition, the growth of the phenomena is alleged to follow a definite pattern: raps, then touches, then breezes, followed eventually by full-blown telekinesis. Our sittings followed that ritual, a pattern that only Robin, Raymond, and I were fully cognizant of. At the April 28 sitting, fifteen minutes after we began the entire circle heard a loud wooden rap which seemed to come from the center of the group. This was followed shortly by an odd odor described by Raymond and A.G. as similar to wood alcohol. None of the other sitters smelled it. (I myself have very bad sinuses which would immediately have kept me from smelling anything. Raymond has a very acute sense of smell. I do not know about A.G.) Right before the end of the sitting, G.L. reported our first breeze—a cool soft air current that was strong enough to penetrate her clothing.

The next sitting continued the uphill trend of the phenomena, and we all heard a weird assortment of sounds—raps, dual raps, and even thumps, and one touch.

For the next several weeks we had sparse but continuing raps and touches mixed with a few totally blank sessions. On June 2, twenty-two weeks after we had started, I had my first touch. It was one of the most uncanny effects I've ever experienced. I was sitting quietly when all of a sudden a heavy scrape, as though made by a piece of wood, passed over the side of my foot from the base of the toes to the middle of the foot. There was no mistaking it. Oddly, this "touch" felt as though it had been made from within my shoe directly on the foot. Later I independently talked to Marjorie and my mother, who had also reported being touched on the foot, and each of them described the same effect—a scrape or pressure moving halfway up the foot from the toes. This was an amazing parallel, and this more than anything else convinced me that we were on a fast road to psychic phenomena.

By this time the nature of the phenomena began to change. The loud wooden raps started to ebb and instead our sittings were cluttered mostly by touches and the breezes. At one sitting A.G. was touched three times on his leg in a straight line moving from his foreleg to his ankle. These touches became firmer until by June sitters were being tugged at and had their clothing pulled or shaken quickly. However the summer heat took its toll, and during the months of July and August the phenomena subsided with only gentle raps and a few touches being reported except during one sitting when the chair I was sitting on was struck three times in succession by something invisible.

We were now entering September and I had to fly to Philadelphia and New York for a week. Unfortunately my absence caused me to miss the first growth of the next phase in the phenomena's development. Twenty minutes after the start of the sitting (again note that it seems as though phenomena begin from fifteen to twenty minutes after the commencement of the séance), Raymond, A.G., and Marjorie heard slight whistling sounds emanating from shoulder height in the circle. They were distinct and measured with pauses between them. I returned the next week and it was as if the "force" was acknowledging my return, for the only manifestation that night was a touch on my left side right after we began the séance. The next week was a dead blank, but at the subsequent sittings things got jumping again.

This sitting of September 22 was the most unique and phenomenal of the series. Robin, A.G., and G.L. were all on vacation. Marjorie phoned to say that Raymond was ill and that perhaps we should cancel the sitting. I urged that since we had not canceled in thirty-eight weeks we should go on no matter how few sitters were present; Marjorie agreed. Raymond was able to join us at the last minute, but we still only sat with four people, so we removed the extra chairs and began. Ten minutes after we started we all heard the loudest raps we had encountered. They came every few minutes in a startling array of sound and volume. This night was the coolest we had had during the summer. The raps were at times so loud that we could only imitate some of them by firmly hitting the back of one of the metal chairs with a pair of scissors, clanging it noisily.

The next week we had only three sitters since Raymond was still ill, but we did achieve a few raps.

Unfortunately October brought with it a subsidence of the manifestations. The touches became more infrequent and for several weeks we only got raps and even these were produced sparingly. We had several totally blank sessions as well, which was discouraging in light of what had gone before. This drought lasted for some time, and it soon became obvious to us that our home circle had reached its pinnacle, that we just could not develop any further, and that the sittings were beginning a downward trend. So after one year of steady and dedicated experimentation, we decided to disband. We had achieved our aim of inducing some minor PK effects, but we had failed to achieve the movement of objects or other physical phenomena we had set as our goal.

Even if our sittings were a curious mixture of success and failure, they were instructive. They did demonstrate that the old Spiritualist doctrines, which are all but forgotten by psychical research today due to its retreat to the laboratory, may have cogent value to the psychical investigator. The fact that these procedures did produce minor but distinct telekinetic effects also makes me inclined to believe that reports from other home circles recording extremely violent displays of physical phenomena are not at all unbelievable. If we could produce raps, breezes, and touches, others could easily have witnessed levitations, movement of objects, and even voices.

Reading over the notes of these sittings four years after their conclusion is also illustrative. The phenomena followed a consistent pattern. Utter silence and failure gradually grew into raps; the raps gave way to touches, and from touches to breezes. The decline of the phenomena followed the reverse pattern. Lively séances were followed by blanks. Whatever the PK force was, it gradually conserved itself, discharged, and then renewed its charge.

The first objection the critic might have to these experiments is simply that of chicanery. Could any of us have been the culprit? There are three major rebuttals to this very real danger. First, the sittings and development of the phenomena followed a logical order and consistency over several months. If this were due to fraud, it would have had to be a very-well-thought-out and executed one. Second, phenomena occurred during the absence of each one of us. If the effects we recorded were due to fraud, it would have had to be by several of the participants. Lastly, we were all huddled together in a small room. Even in the pitch-blackness no member of the group could have made a move without being detected by other members. In the same context, many of the raps were produced outside the circle, and outside the range of anyone's hands or feet. Could we be misconstruing normal sounds? Actually in all the fifty-odd séances only two bogus phenomena occurred which were easily detected. One was the rattling of an object on Raymond's desk caused by a passing truck on a nearby freeway. The second incident involved sounds coming from the room's closet. A quick search revealed the culprit—one of Raymond's cats aroused from its impromptu and unsuspected nap in a cardboard carton! On this occasion we had neglected to check the cats' whereabouts as was our usual procedure.

The fact that phenomena occurred when each of us was absent, or even in the absence of several of the members, is a startling discovery. It proves that while no one individual may have any PK gifts, the joint effort of a steady group may be able to produce a psychic vortex of energy.

While home circles hold great promise for the development of telekinesis, this is not to say that they are above having problems of fraud. The following unfortunate incident is all too damning and shows that even close friends can stoop to a hoax despite mutual trust.

A few years ago the members of a home circle claimed that they had developed table levitations, objects moved by themselves throughout the house, independent writing had appeared within a sealed box on photographic paper, and other typical spiritualistic-type phenomena had manifested which they had photographed.

However it didn't take long for suspicions of fraud to be aroused. By examining the photographs it was clear that the "levitations" had been carefully staged and photographed. Wires could vaguely be seen holding up levitated objects, and even a hook was discernible on another. This was so damning that one wonders if the reported séance-room phenomena had any element of genuineness. The answer to that came when the group was investigated. As soon as the lights were out, one woman began clicking her shoe heel against her chair, claiming they were raps. A table levitated, accomplished merely by another member lifting it with his hand—hardly very original. The table rocked backward and forward but always propelled from the sitter's side of the table. The whole affair was ridiculously fraudulent from beginning to end. One investigator devised a "sealed box" in which it was claimed that independent writing was received. He had, however, booby-trapped it. If anyone tried to get inside the box, it would show subtle signs of tampering, which it did.

These people were all friends and not out for money or fame. They even went to some expense to call in respected para-psychologists. Yet all the while they were hoaxing each other and the investigators. Each member of the group was trying to pull the wool over the eyes of the others in a grand, multiple *entente cordiale* of fraud. Why were they faking? Merely for the pure pleasure and challenge of it. This is a valuable lesson to learn in parapsychology. Unlike legal procedure, in parapsychology one need not necessarily look for a motive for fraud. Often there is none except the pure, devious joy of pulling a fast one. Fortunately these people weren't fast enough.

# 5

# Fads, Frauds, and Fallacies

As with most sciences, parapsychology has its modes and reflects the fashions of the day. It is actually haunted by just as many *Zeitgeists* as poltergeists. During its infancy parapsychology studied the prospect of life after death but swiftly merged with the growing discipline of experimental psychology to adopt the statistical testing of ESP. With the great advances in nuclear physics parapsychology too is now looking into the topsy-turvy world of subatomic particles, hoping to find the keys to psi's perennially locked doors.

However, science has always had its fads—from Lamarckianism to "ether" theories, and scientific fads and fashions are no greater in diversity than those found in pop culture. Occultism is one undeniable element; Edgar Cayce cults grow and multiply; astrology has as many waxings and wanings as its own moon; and Tarot manifests a resurgence every now and then. Fads and fashion have a considerable effect on parapsychology which often gets itself caught up in current esoteric movements and in many instances even offers support to them.

Parapsychology's most notable current fad is healing. The reasons for this interest are both social and psychological. From a social standpoint, people automatically turn to healing cults in the face of social chaos. Healing cults developed in the past as a reaction to Darwinism, and similar cults can be traced as far back as the fall of the Roman Empire. In the fore of a rapidly changing society and its concomitant change in moral and ethical standards, people often flock to religion to reinforce the efficacy of their staid life-styles. To give greater conviction to its patrons, religion must offer miracles in keeping with the scientific spirit of the day. So naturally healing cults arise—the ultimate promise of faith over science and materialism.

The psychological reasons for today's concern with healing are no less questionable. Unlike most types of psychic ability, the psychic healer is rarely put on the spot. A stage psychic must dish out a mass of verifiable facts and figures about his client and the trance medium must do likewise for his sitter. But healing is so difficult to verify that anyone can hold himself out as a psychic healer and be fairly certain that, by suggestion alone, at least some of his "patients" will claim miraculous cures. It is for this reason that professional healers have always been the spiritual pariahs of parapsychology, Spiritualism, and Christianity alike. Healers are practically impossible to expose, and people will always flock to take advantage of their false claims and promises.

The enormous difficulties in attempting to verify a miraculous healing objectively are more complex than most people would believe. Both Lourdes and Christian Science can serve as apt demonstrations. As is well known, the healing shrine of Lourdes in France has been maintained for years as a sanctuary wherein supernatural healings have taken place. In order to verify or discredit faith cures at Lourdes, a medical bureau was established in 1882 and since then has drawn upon hundreds of physicians a year as consultants. The evaluations are severe, and in 1947, after a year's clinical examination of seventy-five cases, only six "cures" had been justified as being possibly miraculous. Each year's examinations offer a similar small case load which is given further study. These cases are subsequently passed on to ecclesiastical authorities for their critique, while the patients are medically followed up by members of a free-lance international bureau of doctors. A few of these cures, which include such disorders as blindness, tumors, and paralysis, are then certified as being "miraculous" by the local bishop.

Yet despite this complex procedure utilizing the services and expertise of qualified specialists, an impartial post hoc analysis, made by Dr. D. J. West in 1957, of eleven of the best attested cases revealed that not one case had adequate medical testimony behind it. In his *Eleven Lourdes Miracles*, West showed that in each case there had been either a questionable diagnosis, a faulty post hoc examination, or insufficient medical records.*

No religion is more identified with the practice of spiritual healing than Christian Science. Yet its cures have even less credibility than those of Lourdes. In 1909, during the heyday of Christian Science, Stephen Paget, M.D., personally followed up two hundred healing testimonies from the *Christian Science Sentinel* and discovered that the great majority of them were purely functional (or psychosomatic) and that no patient he examined could offer any sufficient evidence of ever having had an organic condition at all. This was especially noticeable of those claiming to have been healed of cancer and tumors. Paget's *The Faith and Works of Christian Science* serves to confirm the investigations carried out by Richard Cabot of Harvard Medical School who found that most Christian Science cures were of psychosomatic illnesses and that claims of miraculous cures from organic illnesses were not backed up with proper diagnoses ("One Hundred Christian Science Cures," *McClure's Magazine*, August 1908).

Despite these condemnations, evidence for healing is still being pursued by some parapsychologists and by the ill themselves. But faith cures and the laying on of hands are passé. Modern healing has been directed into more glamorous and exotic displays, the most notable healing gimmicks being "psychic surgery" and ra-

* D. J. West, *Eleven Lourdes Miracles* (New York: Helix Press, 1957).

dionics, both of which combine the qualities of fad, fallacy, and outrageous fraud.

It is nearly impossible to judge the age of the historical antecedents of modern psychic surgery. Both Asian shamans and Indian medicine men practiced "sucking" diseased tissue from a patient's body and through his skin to cure a disorder. Even at that time this was done by secreting a piece of organic matter in the mouth or stomach and regurgitating it at the appropriate moment. Psychic surgery today is a little more complex but hardly any more mysterious despite the fact that many people support the phenomenon as authentic. During the mid-1960s reports began to emerge from the Philippines and Brazil of miraculous psychic surgeons who by the stroke of their hands would open gaping wounds and painlessly remove gory pieces of matter, and with a wandlike motion close the incisions, leaving no scars. The patient was "cured," quickly and painlessly. The chief wonder-worker was an amateur magician-turned-healer, "Dr." Tony Agpaoa. Since the Philippines have a large Spiritualist population, his practice brought him many patients and many testimonials. The following is a typical eyewitness report of Tony in action (*Fate*, January 1966):

> "Dr. Tony" took the elderly Philippine woman by the hand and led her to the cot in his small clinic in Manila. The room, 15 square feet, was almost bare. Beside the cot was a table on which lay a bottle of rubbing alcohol and a pair of scissors.
>
> The woman reclined on the cot while "Dr. Tony" momentarily kneaded and probed her abdomen. Suddenly he rubbed the edge of his hand across the conscious woman's stomach and, as if he had used a surgeon's scalpel, the flesh parted.
>
> The 26 year old healer reached with his finger into the patient's abdomen and grabbed a tumorous mass of tissue. Then he cut off the tumor with the pair of scissors, rubbed the alcohol onto the abdomen with his flat hand, and as he rubbed the gaping incision closed. Hardly a mark remained on the woman's stomach.

An observation or an interpretation of what had happened? The photograph of this surgery accompanying the report shows a sheet held close up to the "wound" and Tony's hands obstructing the view of it. For all practical purposes what the reporter viewed as a "tumor" on the photograph looks as though Tony were merely wedging his fingers on both sides of the patient's own flesh pinched up into a welt and smeared with a little blood.

A fierce debate broke out over Tony when newsreels of his surgery began to circulate in the United States. At first sight the performance was impressive. A patient, usually overweight, would be placed on an operating table. Tony would place a sheet over the bared body and begin kneading the diseased area. Spurts of blood would begin to issue from a crevice-like aperture in the skin, and as the kneading continued chunks of organic matter slowly appeared between the healer's hands. With the operation over, Tony extracted his hands and the skin popped into place, leaving not even a vestige of a scar. Shortly after the release of these films Harold Sherman came out with the first extensive book on the subject, *Wonder Healers of the Philippines*, and a Los Angeles chiropractor, Dr. Bernard Jensen, followed suit with a booklet, *Tony—the Spiritual Healer at Work*, complete with some gruesome photographs. Finally, Dr. Ian Stevenson flew to the Philippines and returned to announce that further study was needed to evaluate the phenomena.

However the tide was soon to change. When one watches a professional magician, it is with the realization that many illusions are carried out, yet the performance is accepted as entertainment, not as anything miraculous. Unfortunately people often investigate the psychical in the erroneous frame of mind that if one is halfway intelligent one can see through the tricks of a professional psychic. Many self-professed investigators went to the Philippines with this attitude, without any background in sleight of hand, and were utterly convinced that they saw a genuine miracle.

More critical observers could see the trick merely by watching the films. First, Tony likes rotund patients since they are fleshy and he can insert his fingers into the fat, giving the impression that he has implanted his fingers right into the body. All he actually does is bend his fingers at the knuckles. As he massages the skin, blood begins to spurt about his hands. This effect is managed by hiding a small vial of blood—usually animal blood—or a blood-soaked sponge in the palm by sleight of hand or secreting it under the ubiquitous sheet always so neatly placed right below or over the "wound." Some of the films, especially those of Dr. Robert Constas of Los Angeles, clearly show that the blood is already coagulated—odd, inasmuch that fresh blood flowing from an open wound never is. The organic matter used is also hidden under the sheet or, many times, secreted in Tony's hand or wrapped around a finger. At the right moment this matter is palmed, then "extracted," and the surgery ended. There is no scar since, obviously, no incision had ever really been made. Of course, hordes of patients claimed to have been cured of everything from gallstones to cancer.

Actually, Jensen's booklet, meant to support Tony, is more than damning. The photographs of Tony, if examined with a magnifying glass, clearly show his fingers bent under, not inserted in the patient's body.

The deathblow to Tony's psychic surgeries came in 1967 when Los Angeles TV commentator Joe Pyne went to the Philippines with a crew of investigators including Dr. Thomas Humphrey acting as cameraman. Pyne's subsequent documentary was devastating. Doctors examining bits of matter taken from the patients declared it to be animal matter. Tony invited the cameraman to place his fingers inside the wound, but the cameraman-physician testified that there was no wound whatsoever. With a little additional investigation, Pyne found the butcher shop where Tony was getting his "blood."

The Pyne exposure caused a near riot. He was attacked by Tony's supporters, a credulous occult public, and by Harold Sherman in a *Fate* article, "The Good Joe and the Bad Joe" (August 1967) which didn't ever come to grips with the main thrust of the exposure. However, the credulous were soon put at ease by another simplistic report submitted by a longtime amateur investigator, William Henry Belk of the Belk Research Foundation for

Scientific Studies in ESP Phenomena, a nonprofessional parapsychological group. Belk and a friend of Sherman's, Dr. Seymour Wanderman, traveled to the Philippines to watch the surgeries. Wanderman was not impressed and frankly reported this to Belk who, although untrained in either medicine or sleight of hand, went to the Philippines to see for himself what the furore was all about. Initially negative, Belk's hostile letters to Tony after the Pyne exposure demanding an explanation or a confession finally subsided, and basing his views on the fact that the patients felt no pain and that Tony did not object to having medical witnesses, decided that he was genuine. His verdict seems influenced not by any medical reports but by a subjective personal evaluation, this despite the damning report by his own deputy, Dr. Wanderman.

It was at this time that I had my first exposure to psychic surgery. It was in 1967 and the Southern California Branch of the ASPR was presenting a talk by one of Tony's ex-patients, a Los Angeles dentist. The doctor offered a glowing tribute to Tony, castigated Pyne, and then whipped out a bottle with the same flair as a magician pulling a rabbit out of a hat. This, he assured us, was a tumor that had been extracted from his wife's thigh. He passed it around and finally the vial came to Raymond and me. By this time the meeting had become almost a revival meeting with Tony as Jesus and Pyne as the anti-Christ. It may have been poor manners, but holding up the bottle I stated simply and directly that as an amateur entymologist (which I am) I could positively identify the "tumor" as nothing more than an insect pupa floating about in a little alcohol.

The final straw came when Tony ventured a U.S. tour in 1969. A Detroit audience was outraged at the swindle he was pulling, but by the time all the complaints had been lodged, Tony had made it to San Francisco where he was arrested by the FBI. Jumping a $25,000 bail bond he scurried back to the Philippines. The U.S. District Court of Detroit still has an outstanding warrant for his arrest.

Luckily however, the Pyne exposure and the self-evident nonsense of it all took its toll, and within the year what had been the most popular psychic subject of the day became hardly anything more than a corpse.

But occultism can make one believe in zombies, for just as zombies are reanimated corpses, so psychic surgery was raised like Lazarus by the credulous, and in 1971 the battle was waged anew. The focal point this time was not in the United States but in Europe. A group of investigators from the Max-Planck-Institut, again with no background in medicine, sleight of hand, or even parapsychology, journeyed to the Philippines and fell head over heels in love with psychic surgery. However fireworks were really the order of the day when Dr. Hans Naegeli, a Swiss doctor, reported to an international parapsychology congress held in Campione, Italy, that he fully supported psychic surgery based on his own visit. Naegeli reported that he had witnessed some of the surgeries, and after seeing Tony's manipulation, he himself had observed a cure. One of his team members was suffering from constipation and Tony had removed two stools with his hand along with some extraneous foreign matter. At this point Naegelli's report shows just how gullible he was, for despite the Swiss doctor's enthusiasm, there is absolutely nothing paranormal about relieving constipation by removing stools. Even an amateur can do this. Naegeli had brought back films of the surgeries performed and insisted that the phenomena were real. The fact that he is a physician was a triumph for Tony and brought applause from the parapsychological community in Switzerland. But when Naegeli's report was published in *Metapsichica*, an Italian parapsychology journal, an in-depth analysis of this film was made by another doctor, E. Marabini, who pointed out that the "blood" of the victims must have been at least twenty-four to forty-eight hours old indicated by the amount of coagulation shown that would not be present in blood flowing from a severed vessel. He also pointed out that, during all the operations, the "material" extracted looked anatomically alike, indicating that it all came from the same bogus source. He also confirmed the well-known fact that Tony's fingers were bent at the joints and not inserted into the patient's body.

A year later *Metapsichica* published even more damning evidence against psychic surgery. Sponsored by Italian television, Dr. F. Granone, a neurologist, made an on-the-spot investigation of Tony, using four cameras to photograph the surgery. The massed cameras revealed Tony's methods more accurately than could eye-witnesses familiar with the trickery. The film caught Tony smuggling in small vials of blood which he broke at the right moment to give the illusion that blood was issuing from the psychic wounds. Granone swabbed up some of the blood which when analyzed at Turin University proved to be nothing but colored liquid and animal blood. When analyzing some of the "organic" tissue at the Roman University laboratory, the "diseased matter" turned out to be a lump of salt and a piece of pumice.

But believers will believe, and doubters will doubt. In August 1972 psychic surgery was all the rage at the annual convention of the Parapsychological Association in Edinburgh, and the noted parapsychologist Hans Bender of the University of Freiburg, speaking against it, even brought films to support his argument. Several Swiss attending the conference aggressively attacked Bender when he suggested fraud. After the films had been shown, I gave an analysis of them, showing how the sleight of hand was worked and how a sponge is often manipulated to cause the blood to issue forth. In one instance I pointed out how a sudden spurt of blood was synchronized to Tony's tightening of his fist, forcing out blood from the concealed sponge. But . . . the believers believed.

By 1973–1974, the psychic surgery furore had returned to the United States. The public had forgotten the Pyne exposure and was neither aware of, nor interested in, the Italian controversy. Because of previous exposures, supporters of psychic surgery began to change their tactics. Instead of claiming that surgery actually takes place, they theorized that the "diseased matter" is materialized out of the air. Of course, this overlooked Granone's films of secreted vials and the sleight-of-hand evidence. Some of the cleverer adherents began to claim that perhaps the "surgery" was indeed staged, *but that actual healing* did take place; the "surgery" was only executed to give greater credibility to the patients and on-lookers by conforming to their cultural beliefs and expectations.

This final argument is hard to refute—or support for that matter. With all the claims and counterclaims very little was done, however, to investigate the assertions of healing by the actual patients. So the television news show, "The Time Being" (KNBC, Los Angeles) nailed the coffin shut with its eye-opening report on the matter of "cures" when they launched their own investigation and interviewed several of Tony's patients who were claiming cures. These patients, and there were several of them, all felt that they had been cured of cancer, healed of blindness, and so forth, but when their original medical records were compared to postanalysis by an independent doctor chosen by KNBC, it was found that in no case was there any change whatsoever in their medical conditions. KNBC also tried to find doctors who had certified claims of psychic surgery, and the believers, including some travel agencies cashing in on psychic surgery by specializing in tours to the Philippines, could only call forth one. When the doctor's medical background was checked into, it was discovered that he had practiced medicine only for a short time years before and had had his license revoked for incompetence. The government, fortunately, is also beginning to crack down on the travel agencies involved in this type of activity.

While concentrating primarily on the Philippine surgeons, the same practice has long flourished in Brazil, where practitioners, mainly Lourival de Freitas and the late Arigo, use similar methods but seem to intersperse some degree of folk medicine as well. De Freitas' patients do encounter some pain, but this is simply because the surgeon actually breaks the skin so it will bleed, covering up the fact that no wound was actually made. De Freitas is also very careful never to allow onlookers to get hold of any matter passed off as diseased tissue that has been extracted from his patients. Perhaps he has learned a good lesson from his Philippine confreres. For a completely supportive, though intelligent review of Brazilian psychic surgery centering on de Freitas, one might wish to read Anne Dooley's *Every Wall or Door.** However, the reader who feels he is falling under the spell of Mrs. Dooley's obviously sincere tone might wish to read my own review of the book in the July 1974 issue of *Fate* magazine. A more complete look at de Freitas, with a medical evaluation of Mrs. Dooley's own case, which comes to the conclusion that there was nothing paranormal about it, can be found in Paul Tabori and Phyllis Raphael's *Beyond the Senses.*†

Arigo who was recently killed in a car accident, was given even more credence when an eccentric American doctor, Andrija Puharich, went to Brazil and certified him as genuine. Despite Puharich's past history of making extravagant claims, his verdict on Arigo was taken as gospel, but Puharich significantly has never published his alleged "veridical" report. It was to be contained in John Fuller's book *Arigo: Surgeon of the Rusty Knife* but aside from relying on Puharich's own word, nothing in the book substantiates his claims. And what of Puharich's own credibility? He finally has come to believe that Arigo was in touch with extraterrestrial beings because the world's greatest mass of UFO sightings was centered above Arigo's house! (A totally ludicrous statement made at a lecture at De Anza College in California.) Later, after becoming associated with the Israeli psychic, Uri Geller, he announced that he himself had become the emissary of these space people. So much for Puharich and his scientific judgment!

What then is the verdict on psychic surgery? To my mind, there is not one sliver of evidence that psychic surgery is anything more than a shrewd trick, detectable to the trained eye, but clever enough to delude the uncritical. Neither is there any evidence that any sort of "healing," psychic or otherwise, is attained. All in all, it is merely typical of the humbug that has long plagued parapsychology. In the light of convincing exposures on one hand and

* Anne Dooley, *Every Wall or Door* (London: Abelard-Schuman, 1973).
† Paul Tabori and Phyllis Raphael, *Beyond the Senses* (New York: Taplinger, 1971).

pseudoscientific reports on the other—the believers will still believe and the doubters will doubt, now and in the future.

Radionics does not have the bravura of psychic surgery. It is more abstract, quasi-intellectual, but nonetheless just as phony as psychic surgery's ostentatious displays. Subsequently it never made the splash that psychic surgery did. Instead it slithered onto the scene, was exposed, but is once again making its return.

The pseudoscience of radionics is primarily the brainchild of two independent researchers, Dr. Albert Abrams, who died a millionaire (in 1923) because of his marketing venture, and Mr. George de la Warr, who died much more recently, financially ruined due to a lack of support for his research and an expensive lawsuit. Both these marketeers offered curious "black boxes" which the public was led to believe could diagnose, heal, and generate psychic energy.

Abrams became the progenitor of the radionics movement when shortly after the turn of the century he came out with a machine he called the "Dynamizer" which he claimed could aid in diagnosing disease. It was merely a box well endowed with elaborate batteries and wiring, with an electrode that was to be attached to the patient's forehead. While very impressive to the eye, the Dynamizer's labyrinth of wires was pure mechanical nonsense. The use of the machine involved taking a blood sample from the patient which would be placed on a piece of blotting paper and nestled within the wiring. Another electrode was hooked to a healthy volunteer, and by "tapping" the healthy person and by listening to the sounds made, the practitioner could diagnose the ills of his patient. Of course it was explained that the doctor was reading some sort of "vital radiation" from the patient's blood. This explanation, while seemingly impressive, was cryptic at best.

Man often personifies the machine by giving it human qualities. In science fiction one reads of computers taking over the world or androids of the future learning emotion. This personification has a psychological basis in man's fascination with the machine and his almost mystical reverence for it. True to form the Dynamizer was soon credited not only with diagnostic abilities, but also with the power to determine age, sex, and even religion of the patient. And it didn't need the blood sample anymore—a specimen of handwriting would do just as well.

Soon after Abrams started marketing the Dynamizer, out came the "Oscilloclast," its natural complement. This contraption gave off curative emanations to heal the patient similar to the manner in which the Dynamizer had diagnosed him. The "telepathic" abilities of the latter were superseded by the Reflexophone which Abrams claimed could diagnose persons not even present. All three machines were elaborately strewn with wires and circuits, but to the discerning eye of the electrical engineer, the wires were only rats' nests in boxes. They had no functional use. The dials on the outside of the boxes also offered a feast to the eye. Some had dials, but nothing inside. But who cares, the followers indulgently voiced, the boxes must run on psychic energy!

If Abrams gave birth to the black-box craze, then George de la Warr of Oxford, Great Britain (the town, not the college) was the father of the true radionics movement in the 1950s. Unlike Abrams, de la Warr had a firm engineering background which only gave him added credence. His theory was based on the hypothesis that energy of an unknown nature existed that affected man, and in 1943 de la Warr and his wife began searching for evidence of this radiation. His quest, in fact, was similar to the activities of an unconventional psychoanalyst Wilhelm Reich who was at the same time searching for evidence of "orgone" or life energy. The upshot of de la Warr's researches, which in themselves comprise a scientific comedy for those brave enough to wade through his writings, was the development of, you guessed it, a black box. But de la Warr's box employed not an electrode, but a black pad over which the operator slides his finger. The point at which the finger "catches" due to friction represents a signal from the box which in turn represents a patient's specific ailment. In conjunction with the pad were, of course, the omnipresent knobs and containers for blood, hair samples, and so forth. However, there was no wiring inside the box at all. A guidebook was issued giving a listing of hundreds of "meanings" for the black pad reading which could be used to diagnose illness or psychological aspects. Like Abrams' masterpieces the diagnostic boxes were only a start, followed by treatment boxes, and finally a box that could photograph human thoughts and even scenes from the past. And many ate this up with great relish, and quasi-scientific conferences were soon held on radionics. As the psychologist Dr. Christopher Evans writes of the first conference and its proceedings:

> This rare document merits the closest study as being a splendid example of the kind of eccentric pseudo-science which cultists thrive on. It also shows clear traces of the deep roots of mysticism and occultism which permeate so much of cultist thought. The titles of the addresses range from the borderline prosaic ("The Gravitational Wave") to the more explicitly cranky ("Research Work on the Human Electromagnetic Field"). Few of the papers bear anything other than a passing resemblance to scientific documents in the established sense, though it is evidence that all the participants took everything with complete seriousness.*

And these participants were not eccentrics. They were doctors, college professors, agriculturists, and so forth, who were going to show that intelligence or education offers no immunity against credulity or folly.

The claims that the Delawarre apparatus (as it was finally named and spelled) could detect, diagnose, and photograph nonphysical energy held an absorbing attraction for parapsychologists. Two psychic investigators experimented directly with the black boxes, W. G. Roll and Denys Parsons, and the latter subsequently published his report in a paper, "The Black Boxes of Mr. George de la Warr" (*Journal:* SPR 41 [1961]: 12–31). Parsons set out to investigate de la Warr's thirty-three claims that his apparatus could generate or detect psychic energy. These claims ranged from the ability of the machine to make plants grow better, photograph

---

* Christopher Evans, *Cults of Unreason* (New York: Farrar, Straus & Giroux, 1974).

nonphysical radiations, diagnose, predict, clairvoyantly report on distant happenings, and the "claim to have photographed in 1932 foreign bodies in the stomach of a cow twenty miles away." But Parsons could find no evidence for any of them.

W. G. Roll, also a noted parapsychologist, carried out tests *before* the Parsons' inquiry, but his verdict was a bit more noncommittal. Oddly, when Roll was present, the cameras didn't seem able to function. At first de la Warr invited him to experiment once a week, but then hedged and revised the invitation to once every three weeks. Roll could never witness any of the machine's feats under test conditions. It was de la Warr himself who usually forced the unsatisfactory conditions that completely nullified the value of his demonstrations.

By 1956, though, de la Warr and his laboratory were beginning to receive notice due to books coming out on radionics such as his *New Worlds Beyond the Atom* written with Langston Day.* He was also given public support by notable figures such as the physician-turned-occultist, Kenneth Walker. With the wholesale marketing of Delawarre machines a lawsuit was inevitable. And it came soon after with a legal complaint that de la Warr was marketing phony cures and defrauding the public. The court finally ruled that, since de la Warr himself felt that the machines actually worked, the charges could not be upheld. But the court costs de la Warr had to meet were astronomical, and radionics was dealt its hardest and most incapacitating financial blow. De la Warr continued to carry on his work with his wife and kept fairly well divorced from public attention until his death in 1969.

People's memory is abysmally poor, though, and with the re-surgence of interest in healing, radionics is now coming to the forefront of parapsychological interest once more. And again the movement is supported by scientists, intellectuals, and occultists alike despite, or in ignorance of, its shady past. For example, in 1971, the Life Energies Research Foundation, a small parapsychology group in New York headed by psychiatrist Robert Laidlaw,

* George de la Warr and Langston Day, *New Worlds Beyond the Atom* (London: V. Stuart, 1956).

supported a sabbatical leave by Dr. William Tiller of Stanford University, a physicist and metallurgist, to study radionics in England and in addition offered financial assistance to another investigator to follow up on Tiller's visit.

The following is an explanation of how radionics works, which appeared in *The Varieties of Healing Experience* published by the Academy of Parapsychology and Medicine. It is written by a physicist who is also a college professor.

> . . . each . . . organism . . . radiates and absorbs energy via a unique wave field . . . The fundamental carrier wave is thought to be polarized with a rotating polarization vector . . . The information concerning the glands, body system, etc., supplies the carrier wave and seems to be associated with specific phase modulations of the polarizing vector . . . of the wave for a specific gland. Regions of space associated with a given phase angle of the wave constitute a three-dimensional network of points extending throughout all space. To be in resonance with any of these points is to be in resonance with the particular gland [of the patient] . . . if energy having the . . . unhealthy wave form of the gland is pumping into any one of the specific network points, the gland will be driven in the healthy mode . . . cells born in the presence of this polarizing field tend to grow in a healthier configuration, which weakens the original field of the . . . diseased structure . . . Continued treatment eventually molds another healthy organ structure and the condition is healed.

Simple, isn't it? Is this an explanation or a word salad? Despite this scientific, circumlocuted verbiage, this explanation is meaningless. As the eminent biophysicist R. A. McConnell has so succinctly stated about this passage: "For those of you untrained in physical science may I say that the foregoing terms borrowed from physics, when used in this way, have a certain seeming coherence but are absolutely without meaning" ("Parapsychology and the Occult," *Journal:* ASPR 67 [1973]: 225–43).

In 1974 I followed up on the new radionics movement by carefully going over Dr. Tiller's report which was an outcome of his interest in radionics and his visit to England.

In his paper entitled, "Radionics, Radiesthesia, and Physics,"

Tiller begins by defining radiesthesia as "sensitivity to radiations covering the whole range of radiations from any source either living or inert. Special examples of this sensitivity are to be found in the activity of eyeless sight, clairvoyance, clairaudience, psychometry, dowsing, and so on." This is all very well, but Tiller's understanding of radiesthesia isn't even close to its proper definition since radiesthesia (from the French, radiosthesie) really refers only to a type of dowsing.

The meat of Tiller's plea is that, although the Delawarre apparatus may be nonfunctional, a psychic person may be able to use it as a means to an end in picking up "psychic vibrations," just as a clairvoyant might externalize her ESP with images seen in a crystal ball. This is an old argument. Remember that when psychic surgery was exposed, the new line of argumentation was that even though no surgery takes place, healing actually does. This defense was a ploy to allow psychic surgery to be discredited but still keep it flourishing and in the public eye. There is little difference between that strategy and Tiller's and of the many others who have made the same point—that the boxes only serve as a focus for a psychic's ability. Remember the claim that the machine could also photograph a cow's stomach miles away?

After lengthy descriptions of man's radiational nature, well proliferated with passages akin to the one just quoted, Tiller goes on to explain that the blood sample is placed within the machine and that "the device contains a bar magnet that is rotated to time the device into overall resonance with the basic wave field of the patient." I'll let this cryptic explanation speak for itself. Despite Dr. Tiller's background in metallurgy and physics, I would question whether magnets have this ability or property. This magnet, though, seems to be an integral part of the setup, for late in his presentation Tiller argues, "It is suggested that radiation from the mind level of the operator induces a certain field in the mind substance of the magnet . . ."

One of the most revealing remarks in the paper reads, ". . . an important step in the operator's procedure is the attuning to the subject and the quieting of the emotional self. On some occasions, if another entity is present who is critical or skeptical of the entire operation, he radiates an antagonism that is received at the emotional level of the operator's solar plexus and this, in turn, can severely affect the operator's brain-noise level in a subconscious manner."

Tiller is correct; a skeptical person does cause the machine to "malfunction"—but not for the reason Tiller thinks.

I have gone on at some length on the topic of radionics since it is one of today's most blossoming "healing" fads. Although its claims have no objective documentation or credibility, it does not prevent some scientists falling prey to its occult lure. Hopefully radionics, like other fads, will fast retreat into parapsychology's forgotten lore.

Pop parapsychology's fascination with both healing and machines came to a head in the early 1970s with the development of Kirlian photography. Reports began spreading in the United States about the work of Semyon Kirlian and his wife who had accidentally discovered that if an object were placed in a high-frequency field, a halo would be photographed around it. While initially the Kirlians made no claim regarding this halo or corona, some Western parapsychologists and enthusiasts immediately claimed that the Kirlians had photographed the human aura, a glowing halo about the human body that psychics had claimed to see and which has played a significant role in Western occult literature. Later the Kirlians discovered that if a finger is photographed using this method the halo could be affected by emotions and that the process could detect disease. Another dicovery was that, even if a piece of a leaf was torn away from its main body, the entire leaf showed up on the photograph. This was dubbed the phantom leaf effect, and was held up as evidence that all organic matter has a parallel "energy body" of a psychic nature attached to it.

The Kirlian process can be explained something like this: when an object is placed in a high-frequency electrical field, emissions are produced around it which can be photographed. If one places a finger in the field, the dielectrical properties of the skin are stimulated. Electrons and ions subsequently produced in the field by the stimulation are picked up on sensitive film. This process is hardly new and was used in industry years ago to isolate defects in metal. The whole phenomenon has been called the "corona effect" and is a perfectly natural physical phenomenon.

However, adherents of this new fad claimed that the corona was incredibly affected by illness, mental attitude, and so forth, and that indeed something psychic was being uncovered, since a corona effect should not show these alterations. So, once again they retreated to the occult literature on the aura for explanation. Kirlian research was soon under way, directed by Douglas Dean in Newark, New Jersey, Dr. Thelma Moss in Los Angeles, and at Sonoma State College, California. In all three cases, respected parapsychologists were at the helm of what I feel to have been an imminently doomed ship. All sorts of claims were made—any change in thought will affect the aura, psychic healers showed different patterns than normal persons, and so on. Actually the blueprints of the original Russian apparatus were so vague and sometimes quite meaningless that the devices used in the United States are constructed only on guesswork.

In 1972 I visited one of the country's leading Kirlian laboratories. The visits did little to encourage me to believe that Kirlian photography was anything more than another fad and fallacy. My tour and several subsequent visits were conducted by a young research assistant who was carrying out most of the work. I asked him to explain exactly how the device operated, but he sorrowfully admitted that he could not. Hardly an auspicious beginning.

It soon became apparent that not only was the Kirlian unit incredibly faulty, but also that its operators did not know its limits nor the variables affecting it. I was assured that moisture did not affect the unit. Yet on two occasions, unbeknownst to the operators, I quickly licked my finger before it was photographed . . . no auras were photographed. The assistant was very excited over this development and felt that this had great psychic significance. Even though I later told the assistant what I had done, he maintained that moisture could not disrupt the unit. I again demonstrated by licking my finger and then photographing it. Indeed all we got was a dim outline of an aura with gaping holes in it.

On another visit I showed the assistant that by adjusting the finger pressure on the photographic platform a different-sized aura could be produced. The assistant had to agree. I explained how to make an inexpensive weighing device to overcome this problem which would balance the platform and gauge the finger pressure. Weeks later no such device had been installed, and the Kirlian team was merrily going on its way photographing auras impervious to the unit's deficiency. I also demonstrated that body heat could affect the apparatus. I am convinced that the uncontrolled variables of pressure, heat, time of exposure, moisture, and so forth, all of which are supposed not to to affect the unit, are in fact causing the weird results being photographed. When one changes his thoughts, this is often accompanied by changes in electrical skin resistance and other very subtle psychophysiological conditions. This is just part of what is affecting the photographs, not the human aura.

Yet the results of these "researches" have been published in journals and have had wide media exposure. My argument, however, is not with Kirlian photography per se, but with many of those engaged in research on the subject. It would seem that there is an antipathy toward correct experimental procedures coupled with a lack of background in either physical science or photography. No wonder incredible results are forthcoming. When I voiced my concern over these faulty procedures to one researcher engaged in Kirlian photography, he merely stated that since all their work was "exploratory" they did not need to carry out controlled experimentation. One wonders from what school of experimentation this novice comes.

The final word on Kirlian photography came at the 1974 convention of the Parapsychological Association with a presentation by Dr. William Joines who has been carrying out tightly controlled Kirlian research at Duke University. Joines has now conclusively shown that the Kirlian effect is merely corona discharge and that all the freak patterns that have been discovered about the "aura" are totally explainable as corona discharge. Joines did the phantom leaf effect one better by photographing a phantom rock effect.*

However, despite his findings I am sure Joines will merely be labeled an iconoclast and that those parapsychologists engaged in Kirlian work will ignore any findings contrary to their own. They will go on taking photographs and revering their bogus auras in awe.

People who are involved in psychical research often don't *want* to know the truth. Take for instance the case of a well-known charlatan blindfold reader who claimed to read with her fingers. The catch in her case was that after demonstrating dermo-optical vision the "psychic" and her father, who had trained her in the stunt, would claim that they could teach the blind to read. Having given an impressive show, these con artists were viciously bilking the blind for large sums of money by offering them false hopes in exchange. It was one of the most disgusting con games ever. Some years later I met two young research assistants in a parapsychological laboratory who were enthralled by a case of skin vision. Looking at the report it was evident that the elaborate document was about the charlatan.

At first I was disappointed that these young potential scientists could have been taken in by the trick. I explained that when a person is blindfolded: (1) it is always possible to read down the nose no matter how tightly the blindfold is tied, and (2) there are certain ways of manipulating the muscles of the forehead in order to sabotage attempts to blindfold the eyes properly.

Well, no one believed me. I wasn't surprised at that. So I took a blindfold, had my eyes bound, and casually read off serial numbers of dollar bills. It was a rather nice performance of fake dermo-

* In the December 1974 issue of *Psychic*, a damning report on Kirlian photography was made stemming from research at Stanford University which explains the perfectly normal physical process involved. See "Kirlian Photography Revealed?" by Carolyn Dobervich, pp. 34–39.

optical reading. The young experimenters denied that anyone could do it, and the next week they had Xeroxed copies of the report and were handing it out to the rest of the staff with religious fervor despite my "exposure."

Even if healing may represent a genuine psychic effect, there are still psychological reasons for man's preoccupation with it. Psychic surgery, Kirlian photography, black boxes, and so forth, all represent man's desire to show that his mind can transcend the flesh. Man has always strived to prove that he can master the world and his body through spiritual resources. And the desire not only to transcend the body, but also to control it supernaturally, has led to another fad in parapsychology—the renaissance of fakir tricks and yogic displays.*

Back in the 1920s and 1930s the United States was the scene of a faddish interest in the marvels of the East. A few decades previously Vivekananda, the great Indian teacher and Yogi, had spread the Eastern philosophy of Vedanta throughout the country and soon the mysterious Asiatic culture caught the imagination of the general public just as it had in Marco Polo's time centuries before. One upshot of this interest was the sudden invasion of the United States by Yogis and fakirs, so-called miracle workers, who astounded the public by lying on beds of nails, walking on broken glass, treading over burning embers, and being buried alive—all done painlessly and with obvious facility. Today, we are again in a cultural revolution and with the burgeoning interest in the powers of the mind, biofeedback, Yoga, and meditation, several wonder workers are once more performing and promoting their "miracles."

While the public is often easily taken in by these stunts, it can readily be shown that walking on broken glass, fire walking, lying on a bed of nails, and so on, are nothing more than easily learned

---

* The following material has appeared in somewhat different form in an article of mine, "Fakirs and Fakers," *Psychic*, December 1973. This article includes photographs of my performance of one of the most popular of fakir stunts, the broken-glass walk.

stunts that can be mastered by anyone without recourse to occult, mystical, or yogic powers. Even well-known authorities on body control through the mind have been boggled by bed-of-nails performers.

Lying on a bed of nails is, like many fakir tricks, based on the simple principle of weight distribution. If the nails are evenly distributed and of even length, there is no trick to reposing on them. If the nails are not more than two inches apart (depending on the body weight of the performer), the total distribution of the nails will readily absorb the body's weight so that no *one* nail will penetrate the body. The trick is, of course, to use enough nails to support the body.

Walking on glass, my own specialty, uses a similar modus operandi. In over fifteen public performances of this stunt, no one has ever realized the principle behind it. The performance is as follows: glass is broken and randomly thrown on the ground. Coke bottles work best since they break into large, curved, jagged pieces. A field is then made of the glass with enough broken pieces to make a complete walking area. Then the performer, barefoot, steadily walks across it, the glass crunching under his feet as he walks unharmed. When enough glass is used, the effect is stunning, and it appears that the fakir is immune to being cut by the jagged, ugly-looking glass. (In fifteen performances I've only nicked myself once.) Like many such stunts, the trick's major effectiveness lies in the fact that it looks so gruesome.

The trick once again is one of weight distribution and is easily mastered. Despite common directives, the glass need not be pulverized. (In fact, slivers of pulverized glass often get stuck in the feet.) Large, wicked-looking, jagged pieces should be used. However, the catch is that the glass must be laid evenly on a firm surface. In this way, although the glass may settle as it is walked upon, it will not slip under the feet. Only one layer of glass should be used since glass laid on glass will cause slippage and is extremely dangerous. In fact, if you ever see this trick done by a performer claiming occult power, challenge him to do it glass on glass and see how fast he hedges. If the glass is properly laid, the walker merely has to trod steadily, bringing his feet directly downward, evenly and firmly with no shifting. The glass will evenly absorb the body weight so that no edge will penetrate the skin as the performer marches over the area. The basic stunt has its elaborations. One can lie bareback on the glass and allow another person to stand on one's stomach without the glass breaking the skin. The weight of the person is important and should not exceed the weight of the performer. If a board or plank is placed on top of the person lying on glass then up to five people can stand on the practitioner for several seconds . . . the board and body absorbing the weight.

This effect is similar to another fakir trick which is even more impressive. The performer lies on two swords or on a bed of nails. A rock is placed on his body and is broken with a sledgehammer. This is a truly astonishing feat but is based on a single principle. The rock itself is usually of a light composition. The swords or nails absorb the body's weight, the rock absorbs the impact of the sledgehammer and it is evenly distributed over the body, causing no injury.

The grand finale of these stunts is the fire walk which has mystified audiences for centuries. In fact, it was not until the 1930s that the procedures upon which the fire walk is based were uncovered. One lively practitioner of this trick was the fakir Kuda Bux who was tested by the English psychical investigator, Harry Price. Here is his account of Kuda Bux's fire walking from his book, *Fifty Years of Psychical Research:*

> The fire trenches were made to Bux's specifications, and at the final demonstration the one walked in measured eleven feet long, six feet wide, and nine inches deep. To make the fire (which was ignited at 8:20 A.M.) some seven tons of oak logs, one ton of firewood, a load of charcoal, ten gallons of paraffin, and fifty copies of *The Times* were used. The temperatures were then measured and it was found that the heat of the surface was 430° Centigrade, and the interior, 1400° Centigrade. Bux walked barefoot over the fire twice, each time in four strides, and at both attempts each foot was in contact with the embers twice.

Of course Bux claimed his ability was due to mystical powers.

Price was intrigued by his ability and soon began his own experiments from which he discovered that if one walks steadily with absolutely no stalling and if each foot rests for only a brief time, no burn will occur if the walker advances a total of only four strides. Stalling or coming into contact with the embers more than twice per foot would cause blistering. Price, in fact, challenged another Yogi to walk a twenty-foot trench, which would necessitate more than the four strides that seem to be the limit. The fakir agreed and was burned.

This however is only a general principle. Fire walking is extremely tricky and there are several other factors involved. The performer must set himself in a frame of mind that he *can* do the stunt. If he is hesitant or frightened he will stall, seriously burning himself. Fright will also cause the body to perspire, and during the walk the feet must be completely dry. Any moisture will permit pieces of ember to stick to the bottom of the feet which will cause burns.

A second problem is the exact composition of the fire pit. Wood embers should be placed over the charcoal since the embers generate lower heat than charcoal. In fact one old method of handling red-hot coals with the bare hands is to paint a piece of pinewood black and slip it in with the coals since pinewood generates such a low intensity of heat that the trick can be done with the least amount of danger.

However, the most important factor is the weight of the performer since different weights will induce different exposures to the fire. A relatively light person (90 to 130 pounds) can walk at a pace of about 0.6 seconds per stride; a heavier person will take longer.

The final pseudomystical feat to be considered is the Indian rope trick. This elaborate stunt consists of a rope being thrown into the air where it miraculously remains upright. A small boy then climbs up the rope and down again.

One often hears that the trick is one of mass hypnosis and that a photographer filming the stunt saw the Yogi merely stand and concentrate while the entire audience was hypnotized into seeing the rope fly into the air. This story, which is often quoted, is nothing more than an old newspaper hoax. As far back as the 1890s this story was being circulated. Richard Hodgson, an investigator for the American Society for Psychical Research, soon discovered that the report was dreamed up by a newspaperman and the alleged photographs were really doctored-up woodcuts. The hoaxer was Mr. F. S. Ellmore.

This story had a resurrection when a book was published reporting that a Viennese professor, Dr. Pilcz, claimed the same thing—that he had witnessed the rope trick and that his camera had picked up nothing but a concentrating Yogi. Pilcz's claim was written up in several books, but no one has been able to trace his original film or any records of his experiments. Actually his account is taken almost verbatim from the old newspaper report previously cited.

A poor imitation of the Indian rope trick was, in fact, filmed by Harry Price and can be seen in his book, *Confessions of a Ghost Hunter.** Another fakir was so spiritual that he offered to sell the secret of the trick to Price. The sum was extremely high and the offer was turned down.

Nevertheless there are many ways the stunt can be performed. Hereward Carrington in his *Story of Psychic Science* offers one method:

". . . the performer, after exhibiting a few ordinary tricks of the trade, throws a piece of rope, about twenty feet long, into the air, where it remains rigid, while a small boy runs up and down the rope quickly. In this case, the "rope" consists of a bamboo pole, rope-covered; and after the performer has shown his coil of rope, he seizes this pole and throws it into the air . . ."

The rest of the stunt is simple acrobatics. Other tricks are used also: trick ropes with metal latches inside which will keep them firm and erect, hidden overhead strings, and so on.

Actually, there has long been an argument whether there is any evidence at all that the classic rope trick (with the boy disappear-

* Harry Price, *Confessions of a Ghost Hunter* (Reprint ed., New York: Causeway Books, 1974).

ing) has ever been witnessed at all. In 1934 the Occult Committee of the Magic Circle, a prestigious British association of magicians, decided to investigate the matter and found that no competent witness had ever seen the Indian rope trick in its classic form. The beginnings of the legend seem to stem from seventeenth-century travel books.

These then are the ways several dubious yogic stunts are performed. However, there are of course very real yogic feats that are not tricks in the literal sense, but that also can be imitated.

Chief among these are biofeedback-type phenomena. Some Yogis do have the uncanny ability to affect and control bodily functions. Principally these are the slowing down of the heartbeat. Although some Yogis can master this technique, anyone can learn it through simple concentration or biofeedback training. Steady fasting affects the heartbeat so that it often beats erratically. Then one can control the heartbeat by holding the breath (to slow it down), or by quick, almost imperceptible rapid, shallow breathing (to speed it up). Using these methods I learned to control my heartbeat, being able to slow it to fifty beats a minute and speed it up to over a hundred. This is a far cry from certain Yogic feats but does prove no spiritual powers are needed to control the heart . . . at least somewhat. This trick can be a lot of fun. I once mercilessly confused a doctor with it who was trying to take my pulse.

Another yogic feat is allegedly stopping the heart. Often this stunt can be imitated by placing a piece of metal under the armpit, squeezing it firmly at the right moment, thus cutting off the pulse at the wrist, giving the illusion that the heart has stopped. This actually was a well-known World War I army ruse used by soldiers in combat to trick the enemy into believing them dead on the battlefield so that they would not be taken prisoner or shot.

I do not wish to give the impression that all yogic feats are merely tricks. This is not the case. However, since fakirs are making a comeback and are again fooling the public with a few simple, though effective stunts, it is best that the general public becomes aware of the principles behind them.

# 6

# The von Szalay Affair

By far, the one investigation that to me was the most important and yet the most disappointing was that of Attila von Szalay.*

Perhaps it was synchronicity that I was introduced to the topic of von Szalay's abilities the very first time I met Raymond Bayless. I had brought up the subject of Yoga, and Raymond had started talking about von Szalay, an expert in all forms of Yoga, who felt his own psychic talents had been to a great degree an outcome of his self-training. Raymond had known von Szalay (Art, we call him) for twenty years and during that time he and others, including Hereward Carrington, had witnessed an assortment of phenomena with him: raps, spontaneous odors, ESP, telekinesis, and a slew of other manifestations.

What was amazing to me was that, although von Szalay was completely willing to undertake any scientific test, Raymond had

* Mr. von Szalay has spelled his name several different ways, and in the reports from which I will be drawing his name appears as von Szalay, von Sealay, von Salay. However, for uniformity I have used the spelling von Szalay no matter how it appeared in the documents concerned.

tried for years to interest established parapsychologists in testing him. He had failed! I couldn't believe it. I had thought that para-psychologists would jump at the chance to test a willing subject. I was very naïve. I hadn't learned that parapsychologists, especially at that time, were generally conservative and reactionary, and would never leave their ivory ESP laboratory towers to look into anything unusual. This may seem an incredible charge, but during the next years and to this day, many of the top parapsychologists in the United States have refused to study or research von Szalay. This led to what I call "the von Szalay affair"—the perfect case that has gone unrecognized.

Who is Art von Szalay? What are his abilities and why was it so important to bring him to parapsychology's attention?

Von Szalay is an American by birth with Hungarian ancestry. Now in his sixties, Art has had psychic and even mystical experi-ences all his life, and it was the latter that gradually pushed him into the study of Yoga. Art recalls that his first introduction to the supersensory world occurred when he was seventeen:

> . . . suddenly one summer afternoon, for no apparent reason what-soever, I felt the most extraordinary sensation in the region of my heart. I vividly remember a tremendous pulsating vibration and seeing a soft white light spiraling from the epicenter of my heart outward in ever widening concentric circles and the whole enveloped in a soft misty haze like a cloud with faint golden tinges. At first I felt a gentle tingling ac-companied by an exquisitely sweet ecstasy which rapidly swelled to a rapture, "untellable" with waves of light and bliss radiating in every di-rection enveloping me from head to toe. While in this state I was not aware of any passage of time, but gradually all phenomena diminished, leaving me in a state of buoyancy and joy for days.

Art was puzzled by these experiences. Being not at all religious he had little knowledge that these experiences were typical of the classic mystical experiences of the saints. Richard Rolle, St. Theresa of Avila, and so many more have all recorded the ecstatic vistas they entered during their religious contemplation. However this experience is not reserved for mystics alone. In 1901 a Canadian physician, Richard Maurice Bucke, published his epoch-making *Cosmic Consciousness* in which he showed that not only do great religious leaders have this enlightening experience, but also that even everyday people might suddenly have it. Another great thinker of that era, William James, also wrote up his lectures on the same subject into a pioneering work, *The Varieties of Religious Experience*. Art's encounter was a classic, almost textbook case of mystical experience. A modern student, W. T. Stace, has shown that this experience has seven frequently present characteristics—the feeling of being one with all things, that the experience is beyond time and space, that it is "real," is blessed, that what is apprehended is sacred, that the experience is paradoxical, and that it is indescribable.

All of this is well known today and has been brought into the public's eye by the cultural revolution which has instigated interest in Eastern religions, altered states of mind, psychedelics, and so forth. Adherents of humanistic psychology, based on man's potentials to evolve his consciousness and humanitarianism, have placed great stock in these experiences, founded on the writings of Abraham Maslow, the first modern psychologist who took note of their value to the experiencer. Transpersonal psychology has even gone beyond humanistic psychology on the subject.

Yet, that the mind could enter new vistas and that a rich mystical literature testified to this was not well known in the 1920s and 1930s when Art had his experiences, nor for that matter even in the 1950s when he wrote out his experiences in abbreviated form.

His introduction to the mystical experience led him into two areas—Yoga and the psychic. He soon consumed a vast amount of literature on Yoga, so vast in fact that Hereward Carrington, who pioneered bringing Yogic doctrines to the attention of the public by writing the first manual on it in 1920, admitted envy of Art's knowledge and expertise. On the other hand, odd psychic events began to plague Art. As a professional photographer, he started to find odd light streaks and clouds on his plates, ruining his photographs. He didn't know what to make of them and proceeded more and more cautiously in mixing his chemicals, in development, and so forth. Yet these clouds continued to appear. I have seen several of these early ruined photos with their inexplicable light streaks and clouds. Even today they appear on his photographs and are a constant annoyance to him. I once saw an expensive order ruined by their appearance. He also began having out-of-the-body experiences, where it seemed his consciousness left his body. While in this state his apparition had been seen and identified by over half a dozen witnesses. One well-verified case will be discussed later. Art also became persecuted by odd flashing lights, musical sounds, spontaneous ESP, and other displays. He could rarely exhibit these at will, but they occurred spontaneously. Raymond Bayless has been the chief witness to many of them, but other investigators, including Carrington, also were awed by them.

Unfortunately when I met Art in 1967 he had advanced in years and these spontaneous effects had ebbed considerably. His always active photography business kept him exhausted and far too busy even for Yoga, and he felt this situation had negatively affected his abilities. Nonetheless, I was able to witness a few instances that seemed an echo of his former abilities. I used to drop by his studio before his retirement, and on two occasions while we sat talking, the electric eye that guards the front door activated spontaneously, ringing a chime. Unfortunately we could not see the door from where we were sitting, so someone could have stepped in and retreated quickly—but I doubt it. Another one of Art's phenomena is odd light effects. Several witnesses have seen lights, or flashes, when Art is present. I saw this during a dinner engagement with Raymond and Art. After dinner, for fun, we sat in a darkened room with two other guests and chatted. The lights were out, as one of the more credulous guests wanted to try for "phenomena." Raymond got into a mild argument with our credulous friend, and I, bored with the events, was looking down at the floor. Suddenly a soft light appeared by Art's foot about the size of a quarter. It began to move, disappeared and reappeared a few inches higher, and then vanished. No reflection could account for it. Unfortunately only Art and I had seen it. Everyone else was too busy with the argument.

As a young man Art had little knowledge of these matters and was more interested in finding out what was happening to him than in cultivating the experiences. Organized psychical research was going strong in Europe and Art would laugh at many of the reports that were presented in the paper—especially of materialized forms that were being produced (or faked, whichever the case may be) by several European mediums.

Actually, Art's ingenuousness had one good outcome. When he was called for military service he met the army psychiatrist, and thinking that an explorer of the mind would be interested and perhaps have some explanation for his abilities, he told him of his out-of-the-body travels, hearing odd sounds, of his ecstasies and showed him some of the photographs. The upshot was that not only did the psychiatrist have no explanations, he immediately declared Art unfit for the military. A serendipity for Art who still chuckles when he tells the story and thinks of his onetime naïveté.

Art soon gained insight into his abilities, but instead of becoming a psychic, he developed into an investigator and became an experienced student and exposer of mediums. It was at this time that he met Carrington, helped him with his Los Angeles-based institute, and ultimately met Raymond. In fact, the course of the von Szalay experiments was based not so much on what Art had experienced but as an offshoot of Raymond's and his joint investigations.

It was during their investigations of haunted places and haunted people that Raymond became convinced that Art was a more interesting subject than most of those they were investigating. Raymond recollects the first phenomenon he witnessed with Art in his book *The Other Side of Death:*

> On one occasion we were sitting in his studio discussing psychism when a great outpouring of a sweet scent occurred. It continued for perhaps a few minutes and, in searching for the source of the scent, I discovered that it actually came from Mr. von Szalay's chest. He opened his shirt at my request, and I was able to determine that it was pouring

from a small area on his chest exactly as though a faucet which provided scent had been turned on. The odor became so powerful that his entire studio became saturated with it. Then, as suddenly as it came, it ceased.

The odor in the room dissipated in a matter of seconds, something impossible if it had been perfume.

This was only one of hundreds of incidents Raymond experienced with Art. The climax to these experiences was on February 5, 1955, when Raymond was able to verify one of Art's astral projections or out-of-the-body experiences. As he reports in his *Experiences of a Psychical Researcher*:

> Mr. von Szalay insists that he is capable of "astral projection" and has described his out-of-body excursions for as many years as I have known him. . . .
>
> I had these claims verified in a very dramatic way at 6:15 P.M. on February 5, 1955 when I was seated on a couch in my bedroom tying my shoelaces. I saw a flickering motion before me, and I looked away thinking it was my cat, looked back, and saw a curious shadow in front of me which was trapezoidal in shape. Roughly the height of a man, it leaned from the perpendicular at an angle of about twenty-five degrees to my right, and "floated" in the air. It had a space of about one foot between it and the floor.
>
> I watched it in astonishment and, as I did, the shadow rushed out of the room through two open glass doors into the front room and immediately disappeared.
>
> After this incident I drove into Hollywood to Mr. von Szalay's studio, about eleven miles from my home, and knocked at the door. He answered and I said, "Guess what happened to me." These were my exact words, an important point inasmuch as they show that no leading remarks were made. He replied, "You saw me." We then discussed the happening and he described how he had deliberately "projected" to my house so I could see him.

It was during this discussion that Art gave another vivid proof of his claims—he was able to describe the interior of the Bayless house into which he had never stepped foot.

During the time that these various adventures were taking place,

Raymond and Art were spending most of their time studying another psychic of some fame, Sophia Williams. Mrs. Williams had become famous through an endorsement by Hamlin Garland who had written a book about her. Garland was an important writer of his era and one of the first of the American realists. His ever-consuming interest in the field of parapsychology resulted in two documentary books and one psychically oriented novel which brought the subject into the homes of millions of readers. Unfortunately Garland's prowess as a writer was not matched by an equal talent at psychical research. Mrs. Williams was a superb psychic who also claimed to have an "independent voice," a voice that was physically independent of her organism. Independent voice mediumship was a very popular practice during Spiritualism's heyday and one that has almost died out today. Garland tried to prove the existence of this voice, but his experiments, though novel, even brilliant, were all too faulty. Raymond and Art tried to test Mrs. Williams' voice, and they reached the sad but inevitable conclusion that, although she was one of the greatest psychics of the twentieth century, her voice was pure stage effect, ventriloquized in an artful manner to add a little drama to her clairvoyance. Sophia Williams was not above a little theatrics. She was once on Paul Coates's TV show and faked a table levitation. Coates was convinced that it was genuine, but then Mrs. Williams's ego outweighed her common sense and she took a lie-detector test about her levitation ability—and was caught cold. This only betrays the fact that while psychics may have some ability or even phenomenal ability, they are not above faking some of their results if need be. Actually of all the psychics and self-professed seers I have encountered, I am convinced that only a few never faked a phenomenon. And von Szalay is one of them.

Despite the pessimistic outcome of the Sophia Williams investigation, other mediums did offer good evidence for the existence of an independent voice. Art, too, lay claim to an objective voice. This was the claim that lead to the von Szalay affair, an immense discovery that most parapsychologists have overlooked despite every attempt to bring it to the attention of the psychic community. The thought behind the first 1956 experiments was simple: if Art had a "voice" and this voice was objective, could he be *physically* separated from the source of the voice, thus verifying it once and for all?

In order to explore this possibility Raymond and Art began joint experimentation in a rented studio in Hollywood. The plan of the experiments was as follows: An enclosed space would be blocked off, either a clothes closet or wooden enclosure, for example. Then Art would try to produce the voices in the closet. Eventually he would come out of the closet and hopefully the voices could still be produced from it. To facilitate recording, a microphone was placed into the enclosure hooked to a cable leading to a tape recorder *outside* the cabinet. Thus anything occurring inside the cabinet would be recorded.

Even during the very first informal tests, psychic occurrences manifested. One of the first incidents Raymond told me about was how when they were building the cabinet, heavy and loud knockings were heard quite a distance away from von Szalay. Once after a long day of experiments and in full view, Art walked up to the cabinet (a wooden closet constructed like a clothes closet) and rapped his knuckles on its door, already ajar, and quipped, "If anybody's there, knock!" He stepped back and while Raymond looked straight at Art, who was two feet away from the cabinet, it was given a horrendous blow. This blow was so powerful that Raymond actually saw the door shaking on its hinges.

The first experiments were carried out in November of 1956 with Art and a few sitters inside the cabinet. Raps and a few voices were heard, as well as whistles. Gradually the voices became clearer and were always taped as well, sometimes being audible to those in the closet. By December some surprising results were obtained. The key sitting was held on December 5. Von Szalay sat alone within the cabinet; however, a microphone and speaker system were placed inside the cabinet in a speaking trumpet suspended from the ceiling. Raymond monitored the tape recorder and a loudspeaker outside the cabinet. The loudspeaker was introduced so that anything produced inside the cabinet could be heard outside. In the past, whistles and rappings had been heard whether or not von Szalay was in the cabinet. Art entered the cabinet and sat for fifteen minutes saying not a word. Neither he nor Raymond heard anything, so Art left the cabinet. However when the tape was replayed, a very loud voice could be heard to say, "This is G."

Now, although this voice was taped from the cabinet, no one heard it inside. Either the voice was produced right in front of the microphone out of earshot of the speaker or sitters, or was impressed directly onto the tape. Ultimately the first explanation was proved to be correct. If the microphone is blocked, no voices are produced. Even to this day, although many voices are caught on tape which cannot be heard otherwise, on several occasions independent voices have been audible. I have heard them on two occasions. This is an important point, for it offsets the shallow and hackneyed criticism that fragments of radio conversations are being picked up or that we are projecting our own thoughts onto the white noise of the tape, thus literally hallucinating ourselves into hearing voices on the tapes.

Listening to the "This is G." voice today, almost twenty years after it had been produced, is still awesome. The voice is loud. It sounds just as though someone had picked up the microphone and had spoken directly into it. It certainly is not Art's voice. It speaks quickly, almost frantically, almost mechanically, but the most important quality is its loudness. There can be no mistake about its meaning.

Later during that same experiment an even more impressive manifestation took place. Art and Raymond decided to test the amplifying system: ". . . we decided to make certain tests of the amplifying system and both stood a few feet from the closet door and each other in full light, while von Szalay made single whistles at short intervals. I was listening to the speaker when I suddenly realized that we were receiving low single whistles in answer. I then told von Szalay when to whistle and each time answering whistles were heard. This occurred for at least six or seven times. At the end of this sequence, in answer to single whistles, double whistles replied and the last note of each double whistle was lower than the first note . . ."

Now absolutely no one was in the cabinet at all and the lights were fully ablaze. The evening ended with von Szalay reentering the cabinet with another sitter, and more whistles and tiny voices and raps were heard.

This procedure was used for several of the experiments, bringing loud voices either heard audibly or picked up by the tape recorder.

By April 1957 the experiments had taken on a new dimension. By this time hundreds of voices had been recorded under watertight conditions. There was no doubt that von Szalay could produce an independent voice and that the voice was recordable. However the main focus was again to separate Art from the source of the voices. In April Raymond had developed the next phase in his work. A microphone inside a trumpet was placed in a cardboard box, $15'' \times 4\frac{1}{2}''$, which was then sealed and wrapped with heavy material, then placed in another box. Any voices recorded would then have to be recorded *inside* the boxes that were hung from the cabinet ceiling. Sure enough, at first dull thuds were recorded on the tape, then finally muffled voices.

In June a further modification was made. A cardboard clothes cabinet was procured and placed in the middle of the floor. The microphone and other paraphernalia were placed inside the closet while Raymond and Art sat outside. Now Art was completely separated from the microphone and loudspeaker. After a few moments three voices were recorded. Significantly one voice was so loud that Raymond and Art could hear it directly over the loudspeaker. This proved that the voices were emanating from the cabinet, physically independent of von Szalay.

Another odd turn of events had arisen by this time—the voices could answer questions, repeat phrases, and would call the names of the experimenters. Again this rules out the "radio pickup" theory. One highly evidential voice of this period was recorded on June 28, 1957. During the sitting, Raymond deliberately asked the voice where his brother was. Raymond's brother was a neuro-surgeon who had left Los Angeles to go back East but his where-abouts were not definitely known. A whisper was heard that said, "Bridgeport." Shortly after the Baylesses heard from relatives that his brother had been in Bridgeport.

The success of this experiment is staggering, for it showed that not only could von Szalay produce voices, but also that the voices could show intelligence and paranormal ability.

An equally amazing development came on July 7. Thus far most of the voices spoke in a whisper or were male voices. Von Szalay began requesting a female voice. While Art was experimenting alone, a piping female voice was recorded saying, "Hot dog, Art!"

Listening to the tape of this voice even after so many years is fas-cinating. It is not like the "G." voice. It talks slowly, musically, and even laughs in a joyful twitter after its few words. While the story is unverifiable, von Szalay told me he once had a girl friend whom he often took to dinner. They were so broke that they could only buy cheap dime hot dogs for nourishment. They each vowed that "hot dog" would be a key word for whomever should die first and tried to contact the other.

This voice naturally raises the question: where do the voices come from? Either they are from Art's own mind, being objectified by his psychic abilities, or they come from exactly where they claim—from the dead. After years of exploration both Raymond and Art believe these voices are from the dead. Raymond has said that the voices are often of female and even children's voices and reveal so much ESP-based information, and have such resem-blances to voices of people Art knew before their deaths, that the survivalistic explanation is the easiest to fit into the facts.

My own opinion vacillates. I can argue the issue either way. Art's voices do seem to be like classic secondary personalities. They chide him, call him names, humorous and obscene, often curse, offer flippant statements, and so forth. Subconsciously produced personalities, caused either by hypnotic suggestion or mental aberration, show these same qualities. Yet the voices claim to be the dead and to have knowledge of extrasensory things. Whatever their source, it will be hard to isolate it, but my own personal opinion based on my work with Art is that the survivalistic explanation seems to incorporate the facts easier than any other.

All during the time of these early experiments Art was still producing a mass of physical phenomena, well witnessed by his friends and experimenters.

By 1958 Raymond felt that so much data had been uncovered that it would be proper for them to begin publicizing their findings. The naïve world of 1958 was not the choice year for such a startling revelation, though. The world had been wracked by the Korean conflict and was now sleeping during the peaceful Eisenhower years. Parapsychology was a subject sill looked upon as a bastard science at best. The general public wouldn't be interested, but as mentioned earlier the parapsychological community was hardly any more receptive. At first it was Raymond's plan to invite other parapsychologists to verify his work with von Szalay. The results of such an attempt were abortive to say the least. Since Raymond was in constant contact with J. B. Rhine who was following Raymond's work with von Szalay as well as his poltergeist investigations (which later became the basis for his fine book, *The Enigma of the Poltergeist*), he was a logical choice. He was the dean of U.S. parapsychology who had jeopardized his academic career and respectability by not only declaring that ESP exists, but also that mind over matter exists as well. Rhine was the first to be invited to test von Szalay, but he refused saying that he felt von Szalay's talents were not within the range of his expertise and that he wouldn't know exactly how to approach the investigation.

The next to be approached was Dr. Karlis Osis, a Latvian-born psychologist who had come to the United States and made a name for himself as an associate of Rhine's in Durham. He became research coordinator for the Parapsychology Foundation and later became director of research for the American Society for Psychical

Research. Would Osis, so entrenched in psychical matters, jump at the opportunity to witness von Szalay's gifts? And von Szalay was a perfect subject—he would undergo any tests, under any conditions, even point out precautions and pitfalls himself. He was a fanatic on this. Art once wrote me, "I'd insist on real ironclad conditions . . . I'd want the closet and surrounding area completely and positively DEBUGGED by experts [electronic] so there would be no weaseling later. In fact I would demand more rigid controls and monitoring than they would probably ask for. The voices are 100% supernormal . . . and the investigators must do everything humanly possible to eliminate doubt as to their reality by setting up 100% fool-proof conditions, otherwise the whole thing would be a complete waste of my time and theirs . . ." But Osis wrote back simply that the results could be due to various natural causes. It seemed to Bayless and von Szalay that they had reached another dead end.

Actually the Rhine-Osis reaction was predictable. Years later the psychoanalyst Dr. Jule Eisenbud discovered Ted Serios and brought him to parapsychology's attention. Serios had the ability to impress images onto photographic film. Parapsychology wasn't ready for this either. It had finally achieved a respectful hearing for its ESP results, why blow the deal with someone as controversial as Serios? Or von Szalay for that matter? Both Rhine and Osis were offered chances to study Serios, but Rhine's opinion was that Serios' personal habits were so irresponsible that his Foundation for Research on the Nature of Man could not take the time to play baby-sitter to an overgrown delinquent. This seems rather a shame when a scientific breakthrough may be staring one in the face.

Despite these setbacks in the von Szalay affair, there was still the published word. The obvious place would be a report on the research in a technical parapsychological journal. Raymond approached the most notable of these, the *Journal* of the American Society for Psychical Research, through its editor, Mrs. Laura Dale. This was an obvious choice since the *Journal* had previously published a paper by Raymond, and he had informally looked into cases in California that the ASPR was interested in. Mrs. Dale suggested that the controversial nature of the von Szalay phenomena was such that instead of a formal paper the results should be published as a lengthy letter to the editor. The main reason Mrs. Dale offered was that the type of report Raymond had to offer should be promoted in such a way that it would get as much feedback as possible about the experiments. However, there may have been other unspoken thoughts behind this suggestion. For one thing, it would keep the report semi-independent from the rest of the *Journal* and ASPR approval since a publications committee would have to screen all formal contributions. Whatever the case the Bayless–von Szalay discoveries were published in the January 1959 issue as a lengthy letter to the editor. The paper gave the history of the voice experiments, their main results, the experimental procedures, and all other pertinent facts in an abbreviated presentation.

Raymond had hoped for some response, as had Mrs. Dale, but the report went unnoticed. In fact after publication neither Raymond or Art received as much as one query on the research. It was as though the report had never been issued at all, or that a great conspiracy of silence had infected parapsychology. Even though parapsychologists in the 1950s were crying for subjects, von Szalay's voice was, not to be too corny, a voice in the wilderness—and a paranormal one at that.

Despite the lack of any interest on the part of parapsychologists, Raymond and Art were able to arouse some public interest. This lead to a few television interviews. In 1961 the most dramatic of these offered yet another line of support for von Szalay's work. As I said earlier, Sophia Williams could trick the senses but not the cold mechanics of the polygraph or lie detector. A syndicated show, "Lie Detector," offered its platform to von Szalay and he decided to brave it. He underwent four examinations before his on-camera appearance and passed with flying colors. So onto the tube he went with Raymond as chief witness. He first talked of his psychic photographs, which still popped up now and then, and then went on to his voice recordings. Afterward came the highlight

of this humorously sadistic show—when the guest had to validate
his claims by submitting to an unrehearsed lie-detector examination
on the air. This had lead to some very embarrassing moments for
some guests in the past. The following is part of the most pertinent
exchange during the examination:

> Q. Is the tape-recorded voice you have played for us—which said,
> "This is G."—a genuine psychic or supernormal voice?
> A. Yes.
> Q. Did you fake this voice of "G"?
> A. No.
> Q. Did anyone else fake it for you?
> A. No.

Other questions were asked about von Szalay's psychic photos,
again asking if he or anyone else had faked them, and on his opin-
ions about the nature of his gifts. After the show, the producer,
Ralph H. Andrews, gave von Szalay an official statement from the
show. It read in part:

> For the benefit of anyone who may not have seen the program on
> which you appeared, I would like to again make it clear that you were
> given a complete and proper polygraph examination under ideal condi-
> tions and in the opinion of Mr. William A. Schmidt [the polygraph ex-
> pert], you were telling the truth on every question you answered.
>
> It should be made clear, however, that several of the questions con-
> cerned your beliefs, and it is beyond the ability of the lie-detector to
> prove anything concerning beliefs, except that you actually believe
> them.
>
> The other questions which were concerned with whether or not you
> used trickery or fakery in the strange photographs and recordings you
> have were more proper for the lie-detector, in that we could definitely
> determine you were telling the truth and had not used trickery or fa-
> kery.

Articles soon appeared on the von Szalay–Bayless work—in *Fate*,
England's *Psychic News*, *Borderland*, and others, but they encouraged
nothing but doubt; strange voices coming from empty closets, in-

deed! Perhaps it was this doubt that pervaded all parapsychology. So the ASPR report slept, parapsychologists slept, and the public slept. The proverbial rude awakening did not come until another investigator in Germany made similar claims and received much more attention on infinitely weaker evidence. But that is a story yet to come.

By the early sixties research with von Szalay had come to a standstill. Raymond and Art were discouraged by the lack of attention given to their work, research funds were scarce, von Szalay had his photography business to care for, and Raymond had his profession as an artist to pursue. During the period of the von Szalay experiments Raymond had married, thus adding further responsibilities, and he was beginning to turn more and more to investigating poltergeists and hauntings. Although experiments were still going on all this time, the final blow came in 1964 when Raymond was struck by a severe illness which incapacitated him and kept him from psychical research for two years. Art married for a second time and started a family. (He had been married briefly when a very young man and had a son Edson who died mysteriously. The name Edson is often recorded on the tapes.) By the time Raymond had completely recovered, he and Art had gone their separate ways, and when I met Raymond in 1967 he had not seen Art in three years.

It is at this point that I made my entrance into the von Szalay affair. All the foregoing was the background I drew upon in my attempt to experiment directly with von Szalay and achieve for him the hearing that years before Raymond had tried so hard to do. Raymond was reluctant about working with Art again but gave me every encouragement. Unfortunately Raymond did not know how to get in touch with him. So my first venture was to seek him out. I finally located him by an obvious method—looking in the telephone book. Art was living close by in the same suburb of Los Angeles as I was in a section of the San Fernando Valley. So in 1967 I met von Szalay by simply walking up to his apartment door and knocking. He was shortish, heavyset, bald, clean-shaven, and obviously older than Raymond. He was polite, took my name and address and said he would phone me after the holidays. It was close to the fourth of July. Art did call me a week later and we spoke on the phone for over three hours. After that I began dropping by his studio and chatting with him at every opportunity.

I'm afraid though that my arrival on the scene was badly timed. Art's marriage had gone awry and this upset was not conducive to his research and he had all but given up his voice sittings. The years had taken their toll and most of his spontaneous physical phenomena had petered out. He still got voices, but they were marginal, often mere whispers, and his preoccupation with his personal affairs blocked full-scale research. He was still enthusiastic, however, about new experimentation, better controls, and getting a scientific hearing for himself and his voices.

Actually the timing was unfortunate for me also. At the end of summer I was leaving to pursue my own career as a concert musician. I was going to the Cincinnati College–Conservatory of Music of the University of Cincinnati in September. Being in Ohio would restrict what I could do for Art, but I was determined to make a go of it. Even at that time I realized that parapsychology was becoming more important to me than my musical studies.

Although I didn't actually experiment with Art during these months, one odd series of psychic events did crop up which was very convincing to me. It was one of the Jungian instances of synchronicity (or something more) that constantly occur to those engaged in psychical investigations.

As I said, von Szalay sporadically receives psychic effects on his photographic plates. Since he is a professional photographer, these intrusions are both unwanted and financially damaging. Some of these effects are faces or collages of faces. During the summer of 1967 Art had photographed a young bride, and when the plate was developed, a group of "extras" was found at the bottom of the negative. Art spotted them, tried to camouflage them for the prints, but was not entirely successful. The groom saw the faces in spite of

Art's touch-up, considered the picture ruined and refused to accept it. The photograph became the key in a complex series of events. First let me describe it. The photograph (8 × 10) is of a bride in a sitting position. At the lower right corner is a network of "extras." Looking at the photo one can easily discern a large obtrusive head (1½″ × 2¼″) peering from under the bride's arm. The face is male, moustached, and seems to be wearing glasses. Fainter and directly above this head is a smaller one (1″ × 1″). Smaller overlapping heads pyramid over these two and fade into the normal background. The entire column is about 4″ tall.

A week after this photo had been taken I was at the Southern California Branch of the ASPR in Beverly Hills visiting with Barbara Smith, the administrative assistant. During our visit Raymond dropped in unexpectedly, and I happened to have the photograph with me, but at the time had only casually glanced at it. After showing it to Raymond I put it into my briefcase and paid no more attention to it until November.

During our conversation which covered a myriad of subjects, Barbara Smith mentioned to us that one of Rasputin's daughters was living in Los Angeles. Being interested in the life of Rasputin, Raymond suggested we visit her. As I too had an interest in the bizarre Russian's life, I promptly and enthusiastically accepted his suggestion. Barbara Smith gave us the address and phone number and Raymond and I spent the rest of the afternoon talking about Rasputin and his alleged occult powers. As a matter of fact, as I am of Russian stock, Czarist Russian history was a hobby of mine.

At the end of that summer I left for Ohio. During my residence there I took the time to scrutinize the photograph carefully since I had taken a few of Art's psychic photographs with me for study. In early November I wrote Art asking him to send more prints of the supernormal photographs that had cropped up during the past summer. On November 30 I received a packet containing further prints of the photos in question. I still had the full-size original print of the bride, but Art sent me another print from the same series that showed no impressions, a couple of miniature glossy prints, and an enlargement of one section of the photograph that contained the faces (2¼″ × 4″). On one of the prints Art had pointed out the faces. Apparently he too had been studying the photo. It is important to note that at this time I had not discussed the photograph with him at all, and had only seen him twice since it had been taken. Art had found that when the photo was held upside down a *very* clear face could be observed. These face inversions are not rare in Art's photographs. The face was a bearded profile and next to it was a very clear initial R. I had not noticed these effects simply because I had never held the print upside down. Had I done so, these two effects would have been obvious. Letter initials on von Szalay's photos are not rare and is not an unusual trait on the ones he has spontaneously produced over the years. On the print Art had carefully written: "Left profile of bearded man! Note letter 'R'—Rasputin? Ha!" When I returned to Los Angeles in December I asked him about the photo—asking him no leading questions at all, of course. At that time Art told me that it was his impression that the photograph was a psychic portrait of Rasputin.

Here we have an extraordinary set of coincidences. I had been involved with Russian history for some time, and during this time a print with an extra appeared which Art claimed to be that of Rasputin—a figure who had always fascinated me. During the months I had known Art, I had never mentioned Rasputin to him nor had he to me, and the subject had never come up. Yet within one week a link between the subject of Rasputin and myself come from two independent sources: Art's photograph and the first attempt by me to contact Rasputin's daughter. It may be anticlimactic, but I never did get to see her.

Was this coincidence? Synchronicity? Art's precognition manifesting in a subjective impression or externalizing on a photographic plate? I didn't know then, and I don't know now. But it was a rather impressive introduction to Art's abilities.

I spent the time in Cincinnati trying to get independent researchers to study von Szalay. I had a choice—either do the research myself or get a well-established parapsychologist to under-take the project. However, it was at this point that I carried out my own first exploratory sittings with Art. Art hadn't systematically experimented for a long time so his abilities were sporadic and unpredictable. My first sittings were not designed as rigorous ex-periments but only as informal trials to get him back into the swing of things. When I returned to Los Angeles in December for a few weeks, I began my own work with him. For the trial Joyce Vera, a friend of mine, and I sat with Art at his apartment. He hadn't sat for six months and was using a clothes closet for his cabinet. He placed a trumpet on the shelf with a microphone inside it. This was hooked to a loudspeaker and tape recorder outside the cabinet in the bedroom where we all assembled. Art opened a blank tape and placed it on the machine. The experiment began. We did hear peculiar scraping sounds, metallic tinklings, and light raps from the cabinet but nothing vocal. There was a power drain on the appara-tus so we turned off the loudspeaker and just replayed the tape every so often. We continued to record light raps and two definite sighs. Miss Vera then entered the cabinet and immediately the raps increased. When I entered the cabinet the raps stopped. Toward the end of the experiment we finally picked up a rumbling female voice that said something about a "bad day." The first words of the phrase were mumbled and we could not make them out.

A few days later I ran another test with Art under the same con-ditions except that I experimented alone with him. The first hour was futile but we did hear a succession of raps coming from the cabinet. I entered the cabinet and odd as it may seem, I had an inexplicable attack of nausea. On the whole the sitting was a fail-ure.

Meanwhile I was actively trying to cajole the ASPR into an in-vestigation based on all the testimony I had collected from Art, Raymond, and others. I should have known better since Raymond had often tried to attract the ASPR's attention to Art but it had been reluctant.

I wrote about the research that had been carried out, the history of the case, and so forth. The ASPR was courteous but felt that there needed to be a lot of preliminary evidence accumulated before engaging in an investigation. By this time I had edited a dossier on the case of some sixty pages. This I had at hand and I was optimistic.

I replied to the ASPR, saying that I was representing von Szalay and had a complete file at hand. However, the ASPR remained reluctant about the investigation and used the lack of formally published background on the case as well as lack of funds as reasons. It was clear that I was headed for a stalemate, and my dissatisfaction lead to a break in the correspondence with the ASPR over the von Szalay case and its research policies.

During the next two years I was still working with Art, although now running controlled experiments with him. The most important of these was held on October 26, 1968, in which I used my own recorder and tape. We experimented in von Szalay's photographic studio, using his darkroom as the experimental area. By this time the use of the formal cabinet had been discarded, and Art merely used a tape recorder and microphone, replaying the tape every so often to see if anything unusual had been recorded. He also monitored the microphone via a headset to see if he could distinguish any sounds being recorded at the time. In this experiment, we sat within the darkroom, a few feet away from the trumpet with an inserted microphone which was lying in a shallow bed of water. The use of the water was to help carry or magnify any voice. We sat for fifteen minutes but nothing happened. But as we resumed we got our first definite results. My attention was focused on the trumpet, and I heard a well-defined, airy whistle emanate from it. This was a phenomenon that Raymond had heard on countless occasions during the first experiments in the 1950s. I called Art's attention to this whistle, and he responded that he thought I had made the sound, which I certainly had not. We replayed the tape and found that the whistle had been successfully recorded. We sat another hour but got nothing else. Admittedly Art's voices with me were still not up to par, but Raymond, who had reinstated his investigations, was getting some fine results. Finally, though, at 9:00 P.M., precisely two hours after we had begun work, von Szalay asked the "voices" who would be elected President in the upcoming national elections. We heard nothing, but on replaying the tape, immediately after Art had voiced his query, a tiny voice could be heard saying "Humphrey." Humphrey was not elected, but that is beside the point. What was important was that we (1) had recorded an intelligible voice, (2) that it answered a direct question, and (3) it seemed highly unlikely that we were misinterpreting the voice. Admittedly the voice was feeble. But when we first replayed the tape, I was listening to the tape recorder's speakers and Art was listening through earphones. When the voice was played, we instantly looked at each other to indicate that we both had independently heard the voice even if it was not up to the loudness and clarity of Art's usual productions.

Both of us were happy with the result. Art was particularly enthused about the voice answering a specific question. I was more impressed by the experience of being able to hear a voice or whistle independently of the machine and playback. We closed shop and at my suggestion went out for a bite to eat. We returned later and continued into the night with our psychic vigil. However, for this segment, while the recorder and microphone were inside the darkroom, we sat outside of it and completely away from it by several yards. Fifty minutes later we replayed the tape and found a male voice saying, "Hiya, Art."

During the final part of the test séance someone shouted from the street, and we immediately replayed the tape to see if somehow street sounds were being recorded. The shout had not been taped. After the final voice was procured we stopped for the night.

I was able to hear Art's independent voice again at my next experiment. As with the previous test I brought my own machine and sealed tape. At first we sat in the studio's waiting room with the mechanical apparatus inside the darkroom. This was not successful. So we resorted to sitting inside the cabinet. As before, as I sat I heard a loud gurgle from the trumpet. Art heard it through the headphones and once again we shot each other a hurried glance. We replayed the tape and found a two-syllable word or two-word production. Unfortunately its quality was garbled and we could not decipher it. We didn't record anything else after that and gave up trying after several more tape replays.

Even though I was discouraged by the ASPR situation, I still had hopes during this period of getting an established para-psychologist interested in handling Art's mediumship. While in Cincinnati I had met a parapsychologist and I talked with him about von Szalay. He suggested I contact Dr. Ian Stevenson at the University of Virginia, who was particularly interested in research bearing on survival of death and had once suggested the use of voice prints to test any sort of paranormal voices. Voice prints are similar to fingerprints in that they break down a voice into certain patterns just as distinguishable as the ridges of one's fingers.

I wrote to Stevenson that evening and a new chapter in the von Szalay affair was opened.

If a formal investigation was to be made, I had to work on two fronts. First I had to ensure that Stevenson was made aware of the importance of the case and on the other hand I had to get von Szalay in shape. Art was still having enormous personal problems, his motivation was poor, he was not sitting systematically, and his voices were not up to par.

Nevertheless I wrote Art about the voice prints and he wrote back immediately: "Yes, will gladly make voice prints. It's the log-ical step after the polygraph! In fact I would insist on it before I do any serious sitting . . . must be ironclad." However, Art was con-cerned about the geographical problem. With a business to handle, he was not about to close up shop and travel to Virginia for an in-vestigation.

A few days after hearing from Art, I received a communication from Stevenson in which he showed great interest in Art's abilities and asked for information while suggesting that someone in South-ern California do some preliminary screening before he ventured to Los Angeles himself.

A couple soon contacted us at Stevenson's suggestion. We met and discussed the situation at length. The couple seemed impressed. As I had to return to Cincinnati, I left Art and the people to work out a plan. In the forthcoming tests there was considerable awkwardness in the geography as they did not live in Los Angeles. Despite this setback a few voices were taped but the situation was inconvenient for everyone. And just as the investigation began to bear fruit, another case came along, schedules were changed, and the pair could not continue their investigation. Since Stevenson's time was preoccupied with other cases, he finally withdrew without having had direct involvement.

By June, I had also realized that my activities in parapsychology were pressing enough that I should return to Los Angeles permanently. But things were at low ebb. I was discouraged; von Szalay was bitter about the whole situation. His motivation was practically nil. He was beginning to feel that he should go on testing by himself and make his own discoveries—parapsychologists be damned! I was beginning to be sympathetic to his view.

During the summer months everyone began going his or her separate ways. It was getting hard for me to encourage Art to sit. Raymond was now working steadily with him since Art always got his best results when the two of them sat. The resumption of sitting was probably the one motivation in Art's psychic life. I drifted from the scene since it was obvious that parapsychologists just did not want to be bothered with innovation. They had fallen into the same complacency of which they criticized organized science.

Up until 1969 the world refused to believe in the existence of tape-recorded voices, but a storm was silently brewing in Europe. In Sweden, Friedrich Jurgenson had begun to tape-record odd psychic voices darting into normal conversations three years *after* the first von Szalay-Bayless experiments. Little interest was shown in Jurgenson's work, of course, except that Professor Hans Bender had been impressed by the phenomena, some of which were almost identical to Art's.

However the thunder struck when one of Jurgenson's experimenters, Konstantin Raudive, a Latvian savant living in Germany, announced that he also had been able to tape-record voices and had found an electronic method to communicate with the dead. Like Jurgenson, Raudive claimed that, during casual conversation, extra voices appeared on the tapes purporting to be the dead and even commenting on the conversations.

Raudive's claim was little known in this country, but in 1971 his book was published in both Great Britain and the United States as *Breakthrough*. The entire parapsychological community was thrown into upheaval and had to confront squarely the phenomenon of tape-recorded voices. Where Art had failed, Raudive had succeeded. This was also a break for me.

Thus far I had not published any of my own research with Art. In 1968 I had sent a preliminary report to Benson Herbert, who edited the *Journal of Parapsychics*, but he had declined to publish it. However, over a year later when interest in Raudive was beginning to break in Europe, I was surprised to see my report in the *Journal*. Herbert had included some criticisms which I then answered in a letter explaining that I had carried out further well-controlled research. Herbert agreed to publish my second report on these controlled sittings which appeared in the *Journal of Parapsychics* (vol. 4, no. 1 [1970]).

Parapsychologists once again revealed themselves when the Raudive case broke open, for other than Hans Bender who was impressed with Raudive's voices, no eminent parapsychologist bothered to investigate him. But they did sit back and criticize: Raudive was getting radio pickups, hearing things, misinterpreting vague sources on his tapes, and on and on. But no one took the opportunity to test him at firsthand. Cambridge University did give its Perrott-Warrick Studentship to David Ellis, a newcomer to parapsychology, to study Raudive and taped voices in general. Ellis had never done any psychical work and it can be doubted whether his investigation, although generally negative, really demonstrated anything at all.

Most of the criticisms leveled at Raudive were justified to some degree even though hardly a basis to dismiss the whole thing. Raudive was quite dogmatic and not a good experimenter. On occasion he was getting radio pickups. His voices were very weak. In fact his best would be considered von Szalay's worst! Of course Raudive's voices are never heard audibly (in the air) as are Art's on rare occasions, but they are only heard on the playback of the tapes. Lastly, Raudive often does give the voices interpretations that seem questionable. Since he speaks several languages, he often gives multilingual interpretations to the voices. Raudive's experimentation was less precise than the von Szalay work in every respect, but it was getting parapsychology's negative attention.

Nonetheless, a few European experimenters were staking their reputations on the validity of Raudive's voices, and the voices were also coming out with paranormally acquired information. What was more, they often called Raudive's name quite clearly. Even with these recorded cries of "Kosta" or "Raudive," several parapsychologists still complained that Raudive was merely picking up radio interference.

Finally parapsychologists went in for the attack. An article appeared in the *Journal* of the SPR by Lester Smith called "The Raudive Voices—Objective or Subjective." It was the only article to appear and was amazing. In his paper Smith merely stated that since we have no conceptual model to explain paranormal voices, no such voices were likely to exist. This was a ridiculous declaration since we have no conceptual model for ESP either. Smith used the hackneyed argument that the voices were either from mechanical noise, static, or background noise. He had never bothered to investigate the Raudive voices himself but called them nonsense. He also stated that if the voices did bring forth paranormal information, this was merely the listener using his own ESP and projecting it into the static background noise on the tape, just like a psychic might hallucinate a veridical vision in a crystal ball. And that was that. There just was no such thing as paranormal voices. Richard Sheargold, an English engineer who has himself recorded paranormal voices, replied to Smith point by point, showing how he had failed to explain the mass of Raudive's results or the verifications of the voice effect made by other experimenters. Smith simply replied that he wasn't interested in anyone who claimed to have recorded such voices.

The ASPR *Journal* did not distinguish itself in the matter either. It did not review Raudive's book, but people were interested in voices anyway, so the *Journal* had to act. It merely reprinted the Lester Smith paper from the SPR *Journal* in its own (January 1974), claiming in an editorial note that in light of the queries received about voice phenomena "they were presenting this review and evaluation of the 'voice phenomena.' " Now, Smith's article was in no way an impartial review nor even an evaluation, but a complete dismissal of the voices. It certainly would have been proper for a pro-and-con article to appear, but even that was not done. And although Sheargold published a revealing point-by-point rebuttal to the Smith paper, this reply has never been published in the ASPR *Journal*.

However the Raudive controversy did spark new interest in the phenomenon of tape-recorded voices. It was just the catalyst Art needed. The irony was that while Raudive had sparked interest in the topic, the carefully carried out von Szalay research was being ignored. Jurgenson and Raudive were being heralded as the discoverers of a new phenomenon, while Bayless and von Szalay, who had a three-year start on the others, were ignored and forgotten. So starting in 1971 a new series of experiments was begun mostly handled by Raymond. Art's personal life was now settling and he was moving toward semiretirement. Since he was less harried and had more time to himself, his voices made a surprising comeback. Unfortunately Art's newborn wariness about sitting with other parapsychologists was a sore spot. However I had spoken to Jule Eisenbud about Art, but he had been stung badly in the Serios matter since after his elaborate research (see his *The World of Ted Serios**) the parapsychological community ignored his pleas for

---

* Jule Eisenbud, *The World of Ted Serios* (New York: William Morrow, 1966).

further investigations. As happened with me during the von Szalay investigation, Eisenbud was branded an inverse Cassandra. Eisenbud was interested in sitting with Art, and plans were made for an experiment when he came to Los Angeles on a visit. Unfortunately Eisenbud fell ill before his visit materialized, and so the deal was off. I mention this only to point out that even then Art was still willing to be tested by independent researchers.

Since then research with von Szalay has been more or less a private affair with Raymond taking over most of the research. On occasion Art still generously experiments with interested investigators such as Susy Smith who asked for a few sittings in 1972 along with the ex-president of the Southern California Society for Psychical Research, Clarissa Plantamura. The sittings offered some startling results as Miss Smith records in her book *Life Is Forever:*

> In Los Angeles during the summer of 1972 we held a number of sessions which were fairly fruitful . . . One 3:00 A.M., for instance, our co-researcher Clarissa Plantamura called out to her deceased husband Ed to come through to us if possible. Shortly after that we got a faint, high pitched, hurried statement which can be translated as either "Ed is here" or "Eddie's here." As the tape runs on you can hear Art ask Clarissa what Ed did for a living and her reply that he was the musical librarian for M.G.M. Studios. Just then comes the tiny voice again, saying, "Symphony."

This type of extraneous commenting is typical of the von Szalay voices and has been a characteristic of them ever since they developed almost twenty years ago. However, even more significant is that often the voices will make a statement that refers to a distant event. In these cases some sort of ESP is involved. For example on September 30, 1971, Raymond, in a fit of bad temper, told his wife that he was tired of the human race and would like to cut himself off from it. His wife, Marjorie, countered by reminding him that they once knew a man who in fact had done this by becoming a recluse. The word "recluse" was actually used. Unbeknownst to the Baylesses, Art was busy that same day privately making some voice recordings. Art always jots down any results he gets in special notebooks, and when Raymond saw these notations, he was amazed to find listed for September 30 a voice that Art had transcribed as saying, "Bayless is virtually become a recluse." (Art questioned a few of the words but this was the interpretation he gave them.) This type of cross-reference is staggering, and no amount of radio pickups or "hearing things" argument is going to explain it.

What are the new developments in the von Szalay case? There are several. Two of the most important discoveries about them relate to the fact that the voices are physical. That is, they are not impressed directly onto the tape but are picked up acoustically by the microphone. Two different series of experiments have demonstrated this. In the first series two tape recorders were used, and it was found that voices were recorded on *both* machines. In the second series results were compared when the microphone was covered with putty and when it was unobstructed. In every case, blocking the microphone also prohibited any voices from being recorded.

A further development in the voice experiments has been the ability of the voices to sustain themselves. Before 1970 Art's voices, although prolific, could only produce a few words. In going over the earlier recordings, I saw that the longest single recorded voice was made on December 20, 1956, when a voice said, "Merry Christmas and Happy New Year to you all." Now, however, the voices often speak several words. The most spectacular was made in 1972 when Art recorded a garbled voice speaking continually for several seconds. Unfortunately the voice is so mumbled that only small phrases can be clearly understood. What is of interest is that the voice speaks directly *over* Art's in several sections.

A last development is the recurrence of the voice's ability to answer test questions. During the 1956 tests the voices often commented meaningfully on conversations being carried on by the experimenters and would answer questions. However, this trait disappeared for the most part, and this led to some embarrassments since Art hoped to get his voices to make "predictions" that could be objectively verified. Remember the "Bridgeport" incident. This would add another line of evidence to the case. The plan was a total failure, for the voices would answer test questions but usually incorrectly. Again remember that when asked who was going to be elected President, "Humphrey" was given.

In any event the voices are once again answering test questions. For example, writes Raymond:

> On June 18, 1970 I took part in an experimental seance . . . which lasted about two hours. We sat directly in front of his tape recorder, and to our backs about five feet away was an aluminum trumpet propped up on a support with a microphone placed at its mouth. At about the halfway point during the sitting Mr. von Szalay who had been conducting the questioning, asked me to "ask for someone." I asked for the name of my grandmother, and after a wait of perhaps ten minutes [on the tape] the name Emma was quite loudly given. Emma is the name of my grandmother who is dead, and when I asked for this name I was naturally thinking of her.

What can one conclude about the von Szalay affair? The case is now closed. We have proved our main contention that he can receive independent voices, can record them as well, and these voices are physically detached from him. No counterexplanation can explain our data without recourse to the paranormal explanation. Whether these voices are really from the "dead" as Art and Raudive claim is still a puzzle. But the explanation is reasonable.

The von Szalay case occupied my attention from 1967–1972 and these years revealed several things. First they brought home the fact that psychical phenomena, no matter how bizarre, could be scientifically tested. This was certainly no revelation since this had been done in psychical research for years. Mainly, though, it proved that parapsychology, like most conventional sciences, is bound in its own dogma and preconceived ideas. We in parapsychology like to see ourselves as somehow superior to other scientists. We are more open, unbiased, creative, with no preconceptions about the universe. How else then could we ever have entered parapsychology? The public looks at us as though we are revolutionaries storming the citadels of established science in a war for truth. Indeed there are some parapsychologists who do fit into this romantic view. This was certainly my attitude when I first entered the field. Yet now, eight years later, I can see that this was folly. Parapsychology has its own orthodoxy which must not be violated. Ted Serios, Raudive, Attila von Szalay—these cases were not within the limited concept of modern parapsychology. These phenomena were controversial. Snug within the confines of statistics and psychological experimentalism, these psychics were a threat to the stability and current theoretical vogues. They had to be shunned, as in the case of von Szalay, or discredited, as in the case of Raudive. History repeated itself. Just as the parapsychological establishment ignored Ted Serios and his magnificent gift of psychic photography so are they ignoring the voice phenomena—potentially the most surprising and significant development in modern parapsychology. Indeed, caution is a must, and Raudive's own lax experimentalism was his downfall. But with von Szalay every care was taken, every suggestion acted upon, and all precautions secured. But it was as though we were trying to cajole Galileo's critics into looking through his telescope. They were afraid to see and be convinced. As Hegel noted, man learns from history that man does not learn from history.

The von Szalay affair was a tragedy to all concerned. For Art, his once willingness to undergo any test or experiment for any competent investigator has turned to contempt. He offered a revelation, and was turned down, insulted, and then slapped in the face. For me, I ended up in the affair with the reputation of being a troublemaker out to attack the parapsychological community despite the fact that I had become part of that community.

However, there were two other losses. Parapsychology itself lost its chance to study one of the most remarkable psychics of the present epoch. It lost its chance to discover and to advance. For a science, that is sacrilege.

Finally, science itself lost. For the very proof that nonphysical forces exist and that man *might* be able to communicate systematically with either the dead or, on the mind-over-matter hypothesis, his own unconscious via the tape recorder would be a development of Einsteinian importance. One can only echo Moussorgsky's simpleton who laments in *Boris Godounov*, "Weep, ye honest souls."

# 7

# The Odyssey and the Promise

In the course of the last several chapters the search for the unknown has stretched over many areas: from the laboratory to the haunted house, from psychics to psychos, from fact to fancy, and from observation to revelation. The tools used have also ranged from the human subject to the kitten and from the tape recorder to the magnetometer. No wonder parapsychology has become known as an interdisciplinary science.

The search for psychic phenomena is in one way a paradox. They appear to be so rare that we must continually pursue them, seek them out, capture them, only to have them escape our grasp like a trickle of water from a clenched fist. The paradox is that although exploring the unknown is a psychic odyssey, psi is ever present, manifesting under our noses in the course of our day-to-day living. We know that psi is an unconscious process. We experience it in dreams, through intuitions and hunches, through hallucinations—all of which are unconscious processes. That is, we experience the unknown only when it filters into our conscious mind, eking through the subconscious censor.

However, that we are not necessarily always aware of ESP does not mean that it might not influence, albeit unconsciously, our day-to-day actions. The idea that we unconsciously use ESP every day is not a new one, although it has only been recently that we have discovered a way to monitor unconscious ESP. In Czechoslovakia an investigator, S. Figar, discovered that if one subject were suddenly given a stimulus, a second subject, isolated from the first, would show a strikingly similar physiological response. However the second subject did not know he was reacting; only the devices monitoring his physiological state revealed that unconsciously his mind was responding to the simulus given the primary subject. ESP had to be the explanation. In this country parapsychologist Douglas Dean has carried out tests with a plethysmograph, a device that records blood flow to various parts of the body, and found that when an emotional jolt was given a vasoconstriction occurred as blood flow was diverted. This leaves a jagged peak on a graph. During several tests Dean found that subjects showed vasoconstrictions that were not noted by the conscious mind when an agent in another room stared at a card on which a name, emotionally significant to the percipient, was written. Neutral names ignited no such reaction.

Apart from the laboratory, ESP occurs in our daily lives, usually camouflaged in the guise of that most enigmatic and ill-defined category—coincidence. It was the psychoanalyst C. G. Jung and the Austrian biologist Paul Kammerer who felt that coincidences were not haphazard events, but followed an almost lawful sequence. Coincidence was actually a key to uncovering the universe's blueprint. They had a meaning, were "planned," and revealed a distinct force in human destiny. Jung called it synchronicity, while Kammerer called it seriality. However, after wading through the dense forest of their theoretical writings, I can best explain synchronicity as unconsciously used ESP. No better illustration of this can be found than what writer Arthur Koestler calls "the Library Angel."

The Library Angel is that element of coincidence (?) that always seems to guide authors to the sources they need. Everyone has probably heard the well-worn story of how an author searches for a reference, fails to find it, but fortuitously knocks a book off the shelf that opens to a page containing the passage needed. Such incidents are not rare at all, and Koestler has collected several of them which are included in his fascinating book (coauthored with Alister Hardy and Robert Harvie), *The Challenge of Chance*.* Now, would such an incident be chance or psi—that is, unconscious clairvoyance? One isolated incident could be either, yet so many authors report similar experiences that one wonders if each of us, unconsciously of course, uses psi to gather and guide us to information we require.

I certainly am not psychic. In fact I have rarely had any personal conscious psychic experiences at all other than a rash of out-of-the-body experiences when I was much younger. Yet the Library Angel and I are old friends, and on four occasions it has helped me find desperately needed material—each concerning a book I was writing at the time. Once could have been coincidence, but four times?

My first encounter with the Library Angel concerned my first book, *NAD: A Study of Some Unusual Other-World Experiences*, which I began writing in 1968. NAD refers to a little-known phenomenon in which a person suddenly hears music of inconceivable beauty that seems to emanate from no apparent source. Yogis were familiar with the experience and termed the music NAD. During the summer of 1968 I decided to write a book of such experiences, despite one slight problem—I had no case material other than one case to work from. Undaunted I phoned Raymond and made plans to borrow several publications I felt might aid in my project by supplying case material. It was only a couple of hours later that the mail arrived and to my astonishment, here, out of the blue, was a lengthy letter from a young woman in Washington who, having read an article of mine on a totally different subject, sent me a three-page description of her encounter with NAD. What

* Arthur Koestler, Alister Hardy, and Robert Harvie, *The Challenge of Chance* (New York: Random House, 1973).

prompted her to write to me? To send me a case of a type I needed and over which I had ruminated so long and at the very time I finally resolved to write on the subject? Surely this could have been coincidental, but it could also have been unconscious ESP between the young woman and me expressing a need for this very case.

If this encounter can be attributed to coincidence, the next one cannot. Again I was writing my second book on NAD in 1971. I was writing about the possibility that the music had a neurological source since Dr. Wilder Penfield, director of the Montreal Neurological Institute, had shown that by stimulating the temporal lobe of the brain a subject will "hear" music. However, I was arguing that the experiences recorded by his subjects were vastly dissimilar to the descriptions I had collected about NAD. I had just written: "One of Penfield's subjects felt sure that someone had turned on a radio or phonograph. Rarely in our cases of subjectively heard music did any of the percipients have the slightest doubt that they were hearing something that was beyond normal music. On rare occasions at the onset of the experience, such a notion was pondered briefly, but immediately rejected."

Having written these words I stopped, trying to remember a specific case to describe. I decided, however, merely to leave a half page blank and add the case later and went on with my discussion. I had only written one more sentence when I decided it was time for lunch. I put down my pen, went into the kitchen to prepare a cheese sandwich, and was lying on the couch nibbling away when the phone rang. The caller was Dr. Thelma Moss who had just received a letter from someone who had been at her lecture out of town and who had decided to send a written account of one of her psychic experiences. Since the occurrence dealt with music, Dr. Moss thought I would be interested in the case. I was amazed to discover that the incident exactly fitted the example I needed after my Penfield discussion, and which I had left blank just fifteen minutes before. Here is the case as received:

> One morning about four years ago, I was standing at the sink, doing the dishes. I was completely relaxed, looking out the window at the

houses on the hill. . . . Gradually I became aware of some music in the air. It seemed to come from down the hall in the bedroom area. It became louder, and my first thought was that my teen-age daughter had left her radio on, though the music was not the type she preferred, being symphonic rather than rock and roll . . . I checked all the radios in the house, all were off—in the meantime the music became louder, very beautiful, sounding like a large symphony orchestra, yet there was no special tune, no theme, nothing you could hum or follow. There were no instruments I could identify . . . it just all blended together. I was not frightened, but went back to my dishwashing, and gradually, almost five minutes later it dissipated, just as it had begun, slowly and softly.

This case so exactly suited my needs at the moment that when Dr. Moss sent me the letter I immediately inserted it under my Penfield remarks. And there it appears on pages 89–90 of my *A Psychic Study of "The Music of the Spheres,"* with little hint of the strange story behind it. Again it would appear that a coincidence was really unconscious telepathy between Dr. Moss and myself.

Actually, though, these first two examples are small beer in comparison to two others in which the Library Angel guided me through the spreading megalopolis of Los Angeles to find source material. The Library Angel was not merely chance; it actually seemed to have endowed me with psychic radar to find two sources I needed to complete a book. If ever the Library Angel has revealed itself in all its grandeur—like Zeus to Semele—the next two cases fill the bill.

In the summer of 1970 I began work on a thesis on obsession—that the human personality can be invaded and even controlled by the personality of one who has died. There was a rich heritage of research carried out in this country during psychical research's early maturation, and I had long thought about amalgamating it into a book. Finally that summer I had accumulated enough background material to start on a history of obsession research in the United States.

One of the most important figures in the search for evidence for psychic obsession was Dr. Titus Bull, a neurologist and protégé of

Professor James H. Hyslop, head of the American Society for Psychical Research. Together they began the quest in the early 1900s with Bull carrying on after Hyslop's death. Very little is known of his work in which he sought to treat both mental and some physical ailments by having mediums diagnose patients and, if possible, deobsess them. Bull recorded great success as had Hyslop. When time came for me to devote a chapter to Bull, I was in a quandary. The only material I had to go on was a chapter in a book by Bull's secretary, Helen Lambert, and a few letters from people who had known Bull casually. Bull himself had written a few booklets, but these were philosophical with no insight into his research. I knew of no other source from which to draw.

One morning, having risen early from a good night's sleep, I resolved to start on the Bull chapter, giving at least the background of his work. I planned to skip the rest of the chapter, complete the book, and then come back to the incomplete section, hoping to have come by the needed information in the meantime. I sat down to start, wrote one sentence, and then decided I just could not concentrate that day. All I had done was title the page and left the almost blank sheet of paper on my desk. I was admittedly uptight about the Bull material, so I jumped in my car and decided to drive around a bit. I headed for Hollywood to check some bookstores for rare volumes to add to my library, but I had miscalculated the time and when I reached Hollywood Boulevard, all the stores were still closed. I kept on driving, I don't know why, until I ended up in downtown Los Angeles at MacArthur Park. Now why I should drive there is a mystery in itself. It is one of the scroungiest parts of Los Angeles, on par with New York's Bowery, with a population consisting mostly of prostitutes, drunks, and similar assorted niceties of society. But there I was. I had just started walking around the park where ducks and pigeons far outnumber any human visitors when I recalled that about a year before I had visited a little bookstore across the street from the park. The store was still there. I entered halfheartedly, sure I remembered that its collection of psychic books was pretty meager. I checked the occult book section and indeed it had not improved over the year. I had just started to leave and was actually at the door when I saw to the left of the entrance some magazines thrown helter-skelter over the floor. I normally would have ignored something like this since I only check the psychic section in bookstores, but for some reason I stopped and looked at the magazines. Beneath the less than artistic collage I saw a glimmer of yellow. I generally associate everything with parapsychology, so the yellow reminded me of the color of the *Journal* of the ASPR back in the 1920s and 1930s. I stooped over to brush some of the magazines aside and sure enough, there completely misclassified, was a rich, vintage collection of the *Journal.* This in itself would have been fortuitous, but the next shock was to be even greater. As I began placing the journals in chronological order, I saw that one of them had an article "A Case of Apparent Obsession, 1, from the practice of Dr. Titus Bull" by Geoffrey Burns. I never knew that such a paper existed, and after sorting through these journals ranging from 1928–1932, I found two complete sets of articles by Burns on the work of Titus Bull, a total of eight lengthy reports. In short, they were everything I needed to complete the chapter. I bought the journals and was able to go on with my work, finishing the Bull chapter within a week.

This whole incident smacks of ESP. I needed the Bull material, found myself that very day driving to an area of town I have only visited perhaps five times in my life, go to a section of magazines divorced from psychical research and find every bit of information I required. Obviously all my compulsive actions that day were guided by unconscious ESP.

The Library Angel soon became my Guardian Angel, for the Bull incident was matched the following week by a similar occurrence. Having neatly resolved the Bull problem, my next was writing about Bull's successor of sorts, Dr. Elwood Worcester. I had some material but could have used more. I knew that the information I required was in Worcester's psychology book *Body, Mind and Spirit*\* so I wrote to the Parapsychology Foundation, asking if I

\* Dr. Elwood Worcester, *Body, Mind and Spirit* (Boston: Marshall Jones, 1932).

could have a Xerox copy. The very next day I was again book hunting on Hollywood Boulevard. I have a ritual I always follow. . . . I start at Highland Avenue and walk the mile or so down to Vine Street on the right side of the street, hitting several bookstores that maintain a good selection of psychic books. I then cross at Vine and visit one bookstore below Vine, turn and head back to Highland on the left side of the street. However this particular morning I did something I very rarely do. After crossing Vine Street I went to the bookstore farther down the street from the first stop I always check out. This store never had anything worthwhile and I had ignored it for months. But, that day I went into the store, walked to the shelves on psychical research, and the *first* book my eyes fell on was the Worcester *Body, Mind and Spirit* misfiled under occult books. Again the Library Angel guided me to make that extra stop.

It could be argued that this incident was caused by cryptomnesia—that I had seen but forgotten that the book was there and that I was led there subconsciously. However, I have a complete memory of the stock on hand in Hollywood's bookstores since I have gone over them hundreds of times. I certainly would have remembered the Worcester volume. So again this incident must be classified as unconscious ESP.

Psi in daily life is the conclusion of the search. However culmination of this search is the fulfillment of two promises. In 1967 when I first met Raymond Bayless I had had little contact with the paranormal. During one of our first talks he gave me two maxims which I dub "the Bayless Principles." The first of these is simply that if one searches hard enough and long enough, one will eventually come face to face with the Unknown. The second principle is just as simple: that the more one learns about the paranormal, the more of an enigma it becomes. I took these principles to heart in 1967 and today, eight years later, they have become integral elements of my philosophy about psychical research.

There are several sidelights to these two principles. When Ray-

mond told me that eventually, if I continued the quest, I would experience the Unknown, I thought in terms of meeting a poltergeist
or experimenting with a great psychic. What I did not realize was
that he was speaking more personally. That eventually, through
constant association with the world of the uncanny, I would begin
to have more and more personal psychic experiences. As I've reit-
erated several times, I consider myself about as psychic as a silver
dollar. Yet, after a few years of constant search for psi, I began to
realize that my own life started to be plagued by little nonsensical,
meaningless telepathic and precognitive experiences, both in
dreams and in waking intuitions. Before I began actually to explore
the domain of the parapsychological, such incidents never came
into consciousness. Now I can report many. For instance, I had
been visiting some friends and had left them to go home with the
intention of returning later in the day. As soon as I walked through
the door of my house, I glanced at the empty mantle over the
fireplace and thought to myself, Wouldn't it be nice to get a model
battleship, assemble it, and place it on the mantle? I stopped after
this thought and tried to analyze it. Never in my life have I ever
put together model ships or planes, nor have I ever been interested
in them. In fact I am so unmechanical that the very thought of
piecing together a model was blatantly ludicrous. When I returned
to my friends' home the first thing that struck my eyes as I entered
was a model battleship assembled and placed on their piano. It
seems that after I left they had gotten the urge to buy a model ship
and assemble it.

Over the last few years incidents such as this have grown more
frequent in my life. They are meaningless little psi experiences carrying little useful information. I like to think of them as psychic ac-
cidents . . . little psi experiences that have haphazardly been able
to leak through the censor of the unconscious.

Why have these incidents proliferated? And why is it that many
in the field have suddenly reported the onset of ESP abilities?
These questions are related to a primary query that is constantly
being asked: can ESP be developed?

The whole issue is a paradox. We know that ESP is received unconsciously and only escapes into the conscious mind by plowing through a natural barrier the mind sets up against unwanted oncoming stimuli. So in reality we already have ESP, and therefore cannot develop it. What we can do is to place ourselves in circumstances that more readily allow ESP information to become accessible to the conscious mind. We know that ESP is often experienced when in an altered state of consciousness—in dreams, hypnosis, sensory deprivation or sensory isolation, and so forth. When one reports that he has "developed" ESP through meditation or hypnotic training, he is not endowing these practices with any mystical or occult qualities. What merely happens is that the mind becomes accustomed to those states in which ESP can more easily occur. Trance, for instance, seems to be a way of getting the inhibiting consciousness totally out of the way so that ESP can surface. In relation to this I would like to point out two very simple principles:

1. Becoming psychic is not a matter of "developing" ESP; it is just "allowing" ESP to occur more readily.

2. ESP is not due directly to any practice, but is an outcome of a changing way of looking at and experiencing the world.

The second principle is the key. As one searches for and seeks out the paranormal, and as it becomes more and more familiar, ESP is accepted as something almost commonplace—an "of course, it happens" attitude. Such a shift in attitude beats down the mind's natural censor against psychic experiences. As psi becomes less threatening it no longer needs to be excluded from our minds, and more and more it begins to surface into our waking, everyday lives. This is why many of us who explore the paranormal start to have these little ESP incidents as psi begins to become an elusive but old friend to us. It is well known that those who believe in ESP score better in ESP tests than do skeptics. Gertrude Schmeidler, who first observed this, dubbed it the "sheep-goat effect." There are probably many psychological factors that affect this principle, but in part it may be that skeptics merely have a stronger mental resistance to psi that keeps them from experiencing it during a test.

So as one searches and identifies himself with parapsychology, his whole view of the world changes. And that new way of looking at things encourages the manifestation of ESP—which is just what many Oriental teachings have been claiming for centuries. Parapsychology cannot be solely a scientific quest, because it will soon become a personal and spiritual journey as well.

But just as it becomes more familiar it becomes more enigmatic, and here the second Bayless principle complicates matters. When one first encounters the psychic, he begins by considering, "What psychological and physical principles lay behind these events?" There is a natural tendency to try to explain the unknown only by the known. However, soon our behavioristic, mechanical notion of man and the world breaks apart and we are left with a most uncomfortable thought . . . that the principles behind psychology and physics, that is both the behavioral and physical sciences, are complicated by an X factor, and that the world we perceive and the principles we think underlie it are almost as complete to us as is the aquatic world to the fish who cannot even begin to comprehend dry land or sky. We are blinded by the limitations imposed upon us by our sensory organs, our categorical manner of thinking, and the limits of our language. We cannot understand psi because we cannot yet conceive of it in our world view nor explain it by any language we have developed.

As we come to grips with the paranormal and learn more about it, a fairly predictable pattern occurs. At first parapsychological phenomena seem to be a chaos of contradictions. However, the more we learn about psi the more valid it seems to become. Here lies the divine treachery—the compulsion at this time to stop the search for understanding and knowledge and even raw data. For if one goes on with the quest, gaining knowledge about phenomena after this point has been reached, the more the laws of the psychic begin to be plagued by exceptions and the laws that have been developed begin to crumble. I can be sure of my accuracy when I offer my next principle: every, I mean every, principle, law, or pattern we determine about psychic phenomena has an exception recorded somewhere in the history and literature of parapsychology. Take for example my approach to the out-of-the-body experience. When I traveled to Durham in 1973, I had some pretty set views about the OOBE. Not only had I read just about everything there is about the subject, but I also had had my own personal experiences with it. Yet within one week of working with Blue Harary my entire view about it collapsed and I had to rebuild a new model and concept. I had not really believed it when Raymond told me that the longer he spent in the field the more enigmatic psychic phenomena became to him. Now I find myself in the same boat. This is the supreme paradox—that knowledge engenders ignorance.

And so today my own odyssey has led me to a constant stream of ideas about the paranormal. Yet each of these views is marked by an element of uncertainty. I do believe man survives death and can communicate with our world after death. Yet I am not sure *what* actually survives, in what form, or for how long. Psychic phenomena do reveal that the world we perceive is only a glimpse of the totality of reality. But what ultimate realities lie beyond I cannot venture to say. Yet it is these uncertainities that compel us to continue the search through the domains of the paranormal.

There is, of course, one further promise which is a natural outcome of the two that I have been discussing—that the experiences and encounters chronicled in this volume will only be the first chapter comprising my own search for the Unknown.

www.ingramcontent.com/pod-product-compliance
Lightning Source LLC
Chambersburg PA
CBHW031219290326
41931CB00035B/356